SO YOU'RE
THINKING
ABOUT
GOING TO
SEMINARY

SO YOU'RE THINKING ABOUT GOING TO SEMINARY

An Insider's Guide to Seminary

Derek Cooper

BrazosPress
a division of Baker Publishing Group
Grand Rapids, Michigan

© 2008 by Derek Cooper

Published by Brazos Press
a division of Baker Publishing Group
P.O. Box 6287, Grand Rapids, MI 49516-6287
www.brazospress.com

Printed in the United States of America

Library of Congress Cataloging-in-Publication Data
Cooper, Derek, 1978-
    So you're thinking about going to seminary : an insider's guide / Derek Cooper.
        p.   cm.
    Includes bibliographical references.
    ISBN 978-1-58743-214-9 (pbk.)
    1. Theology—Study and teaching. I. Title.
BV4020.C625 2008
230.071′1—dc22   2008020169

To Barb,
my benevolent critic,
my best friend,
my beautiful wife

Contents

Part 4 Post-Seminary Things to Consider while in Seminary

Appendixes: General Things to Consider about Seminary

Acknowledgments

I would like to thank Summer and Sleep for their kind services. Summer afforded me the opportunity to do nothing but create ideas, research them, and organize them into a book. And Sleep actually allowed me to imagine said book while napping. What friends!

I would also like to extend my thanks to Jon Pahl for believing in this book at an early stage and connecting me to the wonderful staff at Brazos Press. It has been an honor and a privilege to work with them, especially with Rodney Clapp.

I would like to express my gratitude, finally, to my magnificent wife, Barb, who constantly simplified and improved my words and ideas. I rightfully and lovingly dedicate this book to her.

Introduction

You're Going *Where?*

"So," she said, "are they, like, going to make you wear a suit and tie each day to class?" That was one of the first questions someone asked me immediately before I went away to my first semester at seminary. I was twenty-one, a little timid because I didn't have any formal training in theology, and praying silently that her question wasn't based on something that was actually true—you know, like, facts! Some of you may be thinking: *Well, that solves it. I am not going to seminary if I have to wear a suit and tie or some fancy skirt.* But before you twist your hair in a knot, you should know that I have never attended a seminary that required students to wear suits or fancy dresses. In fact, I seem to remember some strange behemoth of a man who insisted on coming to school each day without his shoes! That is the beauty of North America: there are as many seminaries as there are types of people. And it is the very purpose of this book to find the right seminary for you—with or without shoes.

Welcome to this Book

This is a very important time in your life, and I hope—should you decide to attend seminary—that it will be one of your life's most rewarding experiences as well. As you will learn as you read through this book, there are many decisions that you will have to make about seminary—even before stepping one foot onto campus. It is my hope and prayer that the information contained in this book will be informative, accessible, useful,

11

and encouraging. However, before we begin discussing the particulars of seminary, I would like to briefly offer a few comments about the nature of this book and what it hopes to accomplish.

The Approach of This Book

This book represents my experiences with seminary as well as information that I have gathered over the years through books, catalogs, individuals, and websites. It's a personal book in that it was largely inspired during the years that I have spent either attending or teaching at seminary, during which I learned much about seminary that I believe will be of use to you. However, my experiences may differ from your own experiences and those of others. I therefore will explain how I have approached the task of writing this book, and what I hope to accomplish by doing so.

First, this book is necessarily very general. It is not possible to consider all the specificities that arise from the hundreds of seminaries in North America or the many thousands of people who attend them. Accordingly, although I get quite specific at some points, I paint seminary in broad strokes and in ways that anyone who is considering seminary—regardless of theological affiliation, location, or program—can understand. For this reason, it is important to take what I write with a grain of salt. Throughout the book I use words like "generally," "typically," and "usually." These are meant to be taken seriously—at a "typical" seminary, such and such will usually be the case—which means, of course, that it will not always be the case for other seminaries and other individuals.

Second, I didn't write this book as an official in the seminary world. Rather, I wrote this book in a very personal way. Although I attempted to be as accurate as possible in every way, this book is not authorized or officially endorsed by any seminary institution or governing agency. Such agencies have previously publicized

This book is not authorized or officially endorsed by any seminary institution or governing agency.

and continue to publish their own official studies, which are readily accessible to those who are interested, and I don't intend to compete with them. Instead, as the title of the book attests, this is an "insider's guide" to seminary—written by someone out of his own experiences and reflections, and not with the express purpose of publishing a formal or official study on seminary education. It is for those who think that smiles, and an occasional laugh, may accompany "just the facts."

Finally, this book doesn't favor or disfavor any particular tradition. I have done my best to be factual and favorable when speaking about specific seminaries and denominations. I don't wish to portray any seminary or institution in a negative way. Nor is it my intention to endorse any particular tradition or institution. I simply share here my experiences and thoughts on seminary in the hope that they will be of benefit to you. When I refer to a specific seminary, denomination, or institution, I do so because I respect it and believe it noteworthy. I have tried to make references to as many different seminaries as possible—with regard to geography, size, theology, and so forth—so that schools and denominations of many kinds may be reflected. Because I hope and pray that people of all backgrounds and traditions will make use of this book, I want that diversity to be reflected in the schools and traditions that I mention. Throughout the book I include the website address of each seminary referred to. I do this both as a learning device for you—to encourage you to locate and navigate these websites for yourself—and as a way to cite where I have gathered specific information.

The Context in Which I Wrote This Book

In this book our discussions about seminary will direct us at times to questions of theology and different theological traditions. For this reason, I think that it's only appropriate to inform you of my theological background, so that you may understand from what context I write. Of the three major divisions of Christianity that we will discuss below, I am in the Protestant tradition. Specifically, I have been involved in what are sometimes called mainline as well as evangelical churches and seminaries. As a result, my experiences and reflections will inevitably reflect my involvement with the Protestant tradition. I assume that many of the readers of this book will be affiliated with the Protestant tradition, simply because well over half of all seminaries in North America accredited by the Association of Theological Schools (www.ats.edu) are Protestant, and the majority of seminarians are therefore Protestants.

Although I am writing as an individual in the Protestant tradition of Christianity, this book is intended for anyone interested in seminary—of any Christian tradition.

My interaction with the Protestant tradition does not mean, however, that I ignore or disfavor other theological communities within the Christian church. On the contrary, I have endeavored to incorporate as many different traditions into our discussions as possible. In this context, I will speak about both Catholic and Orthodox churches and seminaries alongside the extremely diverse Protestant churches and seminaries. Theological traditions of all kinds will be reflected and discussed.

Why I Wrote This Book

Deciding whether or when or how to go to seminary is easier said than done. I've been a student at several different seminaries over the years—a practice I don't necessarily encourage—of varying location, size, prestige, and theological affiliation. I have visited dozens more, and I have friends who have attended various other schools throughout North America. What I have learned has led me to conclude that attending seminary comes at a great cost. And, as I have recently completed my seminary education by way of a doctoral program, I understand only too well how each seminary has made an impression on my life and ministry—and, quite frankly, my wallet. I have written this book to keep you from making some of the mistakes that I have made, and to answer (as best I can) every question that you might have about seminary. I have tried to leave no seminary stone unturned. Specifically, I have considered the following when writing this book:

- Going to seminary requires a great deal of effort, money, prayer, and thought. It will affect the rest of your life. The decision to attend seminary—as well as where and how and when—must be an informed one and made carefully.
- No one wants to attend the wrong seminary. Although there are many schools that you could attend, only certain ones are appropriate or advisable for you.
- Before going to seminary, you must first understand its purpose and whether that purpose corresponds to your professional objectives. Seminary is not for everyone—on occasion, not even for those going into the ministry.
- You need to be informed adequately about what to expect before you begin your first day of class—with regard to coursework, degrees, time limits, financial obligations, and other similar items.
- Locating, researching, applying to, and visiting seminaries are costly and timely endeavors. It is essential that someone who has been there before accompany you on this journey.

Is This Book Right for You?

A student who attends seminary is called a "seminarian."

This book is right for you if you are seriously considering seminary (or merely curious) or if you are already in seminary still facing career choices. It is an encyclopedia for seminarians, to be read through entirely or used as a reference tool. I have taken nothing for granted and have even included a glossary of theological terms.

Let's begin exploring seminary!

ORIENTATION
TO SEMINARY

1

Learning about Seminary

Seminary and Conversations

I remember the expressions on their faces vividly. It had happened many times before, but this time it happened when my wife and I were on vacation. In the midst of a conversation with the couple we'd just met, the inevitable question arose: "So, what do you do for a living?" In response to this common question, my wife answered first, that she is an elementary school teacher—at which everyone nodded approvingly. Everyone loves an elementary school teacher. And then I answered: "I'm a seminarian; I go to seminary." This response is usually met with two expressions, both of which come in succession.

The first response is blankness. If I were to say that I'm a doctor, for instance, people would immediately picture me with a stethoscope around my neck, checking somebody's heartbeat. Or if I were to say that I too am an elementary school teacher, people would picture me reading a book to eager children or helping them with their math problems. But the word *seminarian* does not compute; instead of a vibrant picture forming in their brains, they see a blank screen. And then I notice the second expression forming after a few moments: confusion. They don't want to ask some of their initial questions, because they want to be polite. However, the series of questions they want to ask—but manage to do so only with their faces rather than with words—are the following: *Aren't seminaries where priests go? And aren't priests, like, single? And why is a priest holding what appears to be an alcoholic beverage?*

Orientation to Seminary

In these opening chapters we will learn what seminaries are, why they exist, how they relate to other professional and graduate schools, and why you may or may not need to attend one. In this first chapter I define seminaries, and I talk about some of the differences between seminaries today and those of previous generations. I also note some common careers for students who graduate from seminary.

Seminaries are postgraduate schools that offer students training in theology and church- or ministry-related professions.

One of the first things that you need to learn before going to seminary is that it doesn't necessarily resemble the picture that Hollywood may paint of it. I distinctly remember watching a movie in which seminary was represented as a place that looked like a historic castle, where people were constantly in prayer and walked around all day reading their Bibles. Although this representation was not completely wrong—people who attend seminary occasionally do walk!—most seminaries in North America are not housed in historic castles, or filled with students dressed in holy garb with their hands clasped tightly in prayer. They are full of regular people in regular places. Granted, these people generally pursue holy lives, and theological schools often maintain specific places of worship and prayer; nevertheless, most seminaries resemble other university graduate schools and are not readily distinguishable from them.

Seminary in the Twenty-First Century

Theological education has changed considerably over the past few decades, from the traditional classroom full of men wearing ties and slacks to the contemporary classroom full of women and men dressed in shorts and sandals. Although there still are many traditional schools available to you—if that is your persuasion—it is not necessarily your parents' seminary any more. This is because seminary education, like everything else, has evolved with the changing North American culture. Seminaries in the twenty-first century differ in many ways from seminaries of the twentieth century—which is one reason why a guide to seminary is now necessary.

A hundred years ago, the decision to attend this or that seminary was relatively easy—largely because there were so few choices. The culture at that time was different as well, in that many churches were much involved in deciding where a prospective minister would attend seminary. Although certain denominations and churches are still involved in the process of deciding where a student will attend seminary, the culture in North America today often militates against this. This is partly because North Americans are barraged daily with hundreds of options with regard to every imaginable question: What kind of coffee do I want today? Where do I want to buy it? Do I want it with whole, 2%, or skim milk? The diversity of options available in the wider culture is no less apparent when it comes to deciding where to attend seminary. There are hundreds of seminaries in North America, and there are thousands of students each year who are considering in which schools they will spend the next several years of their lives. It can be a very difficult decision to make.

> *Seminaries today are diverse. Some are highly traditional, while others are equally innovative. Some student populations are mostly male, while others have a balance of women and men.*

The Origin and Evolution of Seminary

Seminaries today in North America naturally have a good deal in common with the first seminaries in Europe and the United States. Today these schools still offer students training in theology and ministry-related teaching, and the methods of instruction are not completely different from those of previous generations. However, there have been many important changes as well. In contrast to the first European seminaries in the sixteenth century, and the first American ones in the nineteenth century, seminaries today are professionalized, standardized, and accredited. They have come to

---

Seminary at a Glance

Word Origin: The word *seminary* stems from the Latin word *seminarium*, which evolved into the Middle English *seedbed*. From there we got the word *nursery*. Therefore, seminaries are—metaphorically speaking—nurseries of theological instruction.

History: Seminaries were formed in the sixteenth century to educate those destined for Christian ministry in the Catholic church. However, the current model for theological seminaries was mostly created in early nineteenth century America by Protestants. This new form of seminary encountered immediate success. At the end of the twentieth century, seminaries witnessed a dramatic increase in the number of women, second-career individuals, and other nontraditional students.

Today: Seminaries are postgraduate schools of Christian instruction that require a bachelor's degree (in any field). Seminaries train women and men for vocations related to the church and ministry—as well as other professions. In this book we will concentrate on Christian seminaries. Currently, there are more than 250 seminaries accredited by the Association of Theological Schools (ATS).

resemble most every other professional institution in North America, such as law schools and medical schools. Seminaries today are also larger, wealthier, specialized, and more technologically advanced.

Diversity of Students

Perhaps one of the most distinct ways that contemporary seminaries differ from more historic ones has to do with the intentions of students today. It's become increasingly popular these days for people to attend seminary (as with law school) for various nontraditional reasons. Many no longer attend simply in pursuit of the traditional career path of becoming a pastor. In fact, it's not uncommon nowadays to go to some type of professional school when uncertain about what you want to do for a career.

66 There was a time when seminaries saw theological education as focused almost entirely on professional ministry. Many students now want to enrich themselves with a seminary education but not necessarily aim for ordained or professional ministry. In most seminaries, this group represents 25–30 percent of students. 99

David Hubbard
(Former president of Fuller Theological Seminary)

I personally know many people who have attended seminary who eventually ended up in careers very different from what they had originally envisioned. They entered fields in business, pharmaceutics, law, government, painting, and so on, instead of professional ministry. What is interesting, though, is that none of them ever regretted attending seminary. And although I do not necessarily recommend that path to you, it is comforting to know that seminary graduates are capable of finding careers not directly tied to the church. Seminary, in this respect, is no longer just for prospective pastors.

Careers Available for Seminary Graduates

If seminary is not just for pastors or priests any longer, who else is it for? What occupational opportunities are available for people who graduate from seminary? There are essentially two extreme answers to this question. On the one hand, a seminary education could result in practically any profession imaginable. I have had friends who ended up in positions ranging from painting to pharmaceutics after graduation. I also know a woman who intentionally entered seminary to become a businessperson! She attended seminary so that she could offer a strong Christian witness to her colleagues in the corporate world.

On the other hand, however, it's important to note that seminary prepares individuals for very specific professions. Principally, it prepares students for the pastorate or full-time Christian ministry. In this way, it is exactly like every other professional school. Just as medical schools train students to become doctors, so seminaries train students to become ministers, missionaries, Christian educators, and so forth. Therefore, any student who attends seminary expecting to enter a career other than that of full-time Christian ministry or education does so at his or her own peril. It would be like attending law school to become a restaurant owner.

Many seminary graduates these days are actually pursuing occupations that seemingly have little to do with the education they received in seminary. They are applying their seminary educations in non-traditional ways.

With that in mind, it is important to isolate some of the career paths available for seminary graduates. I naturally don't take into account at this moment all of the professions that seminarians may enter—for that, see chapters 13 through 16—but I include some careers that many graduates pursue. As you will see, most of these careers are very specific. But it is really up to you to decide whether you will take the traditional path upon graduation or whether you are led to apply your seminary education in a novel way.

Although it is impossible to say with certainty, I foresee that seminary will attract even more students in the future who will apply their educations in unique ways—due in part to the changing culture and technology.

Common Careers for Seminarians

- **Pastor/Priest**: Profession for those who work full time at a congregation—whether as a senior minister, associate minister, youth minister, or teaching minister.
- **Educator**: This is an excellent career for those who want to teach at Christian institutions—whether at the seminary, university, or secondary-school level.
- **Missionary/Church Planter/Evangelist**: Seminaries train missionaries, church planters, and evangelists for Christian ministry domestically and internationally.
- **Chaplain/Counselor**: A chaplain is essentially a pastor outside of a church, for instance, in a hospital or the military. A counselor frequently works in a Christian organization—though not always.
- **Administrator/Leader**: Some people attend seminary to become administrators or leaders at organizations or institutions—specifically Christian ones.
- **(Educated) Layperson**: This is essentially a person who is educated theologically, but who continues to work in a secular profession. More

and more individuals are attending seminary these days for the spiritual and theological enrichment; in this respect, their career prospects are quite varied.

- **Other**: Depending on your calling, creativity, and specific seminary degree, you may have countless career opportunities before you.

Seminary at a Glance

Purpose	To prepare students for a career in ministry or another related field
Requirements	A bachelor's degree from college and an interest in ministry
Length	Typically two to four years depending on the program and person
Structure	A combination of classwork, practical components, and field work
Career Prospects	Minister, teacher, missionary, counselor, layperson, and other

Seminaries Are like Automobiles

Although I have mentioned many common careers available to seminary graduates, there are still many other professions that I will discuss throughout the book. There are probably just as many career opportunities open to seminarians as there are seminaries, and it is one of the express purposes of this book to help you find that right seminary. If you think about it, choosing the right seminary is like finding the right car. Just as cars come in various shapes, costs, and styles, so do seminaries. On the one hand, it does not make much difference which type of car you choose: they all work the same way and are specifically designed to get you from place to place. On the other hand, which car you choose to drive is of great importance. Whether you buy an up-to-the-minute, fully loaded, red Porsche for $50,000 or a used Kia for $500 (the going rate for my 1997 Kia Sephia) significantly alters your life, your wallet, and your ability to actually get to your destination. So it is with choosing a seminary.

When it comes down to it, people's preferences for cars are just like their preferences for seminaries. My father-in-law, for instance, is a dedicated Ford man. If he were to buy something else, he would be out of his comfort zone and most likely would later regret his decision. To make sure that such a scenario does not happen to you, I have taken it on as my mission to help you find that right car, that right seminary. I can help you with this because I have test-driven many seminaries. I have driven the really fast ones, the family ones, the innovative ones, and the traditional ones. I have wrecked more than one, and I have even enjoyed driving a couple of others. I have owned a convertible, and I have probably even driven a station wagon. I have been down every seminary road imaginable. And I want to share that experience with you. So sit back, put on your seat belt, and enjoy the rest of the ride!

2

Different Names of Seminary and Professional Education

The summer before I went to seminary I had a conversation with one of my friends from college. We were talking about our different plans after graduation. He asked me the name of the seminary that I was about to attend. After I told him the name, I saw a strange look forming on his face. "You told me," he said, "that you were going to a seminary; so why does it have the name 'divinity school' in it instead of 'seminary'? Is there any difference between the two?" That was a very good question, and it was my introduction to the different names of seminary. Over the years I have learned that seminaries actually go by many different names—all with various nuances according to history, location, affiliation, and so forth.

> **Seminary Lesson 101:**
> *Do not tell people you are going to seminary until you actually know what a seminary is!*

The Nature of Seminary Education

Whereas the previous chapter was dedicated to introducing you to seminary in general terms, this chapter is devoted to understanding some of the particulars of seminary education. Specifically, I discuss some of the different names of seminary, and I will distinguish seminaries from schools of religion. I explain that there are generally two different names for seminaries: (1) divinity or theological schools—which are ordinarily affiliated with universities; and (2) theological seminaries—which are usually not affiliated with universities. I also offer some new theological terminology, and I isolate several important concepts by comparing and contrasting the educational model of seminary with that of other professional schools in North America.

Seminary, n., pl. **–aries**—Graduate institution of theological education. *Synonyms*: divinity school, theological school, faculty of theology/divinity, and divinity/theological college.

Different Names of Seminary, or Seminary Synonyms

There are two major types of seminaries. The first type is called "divinity schools" or "schools of divinity," as well as "theological schools" or "schools of theology." Some seminaries might even refer to themselves as "faculties of theology" or "theological colleges" (as in Canada). The second major type of seminary is called a "theological seminary." Due to the confusion that these different names generate, I would like to discuss some of these differences. In the midst of our discussion, however, keep in mind that all of these different names fall under the general category of seminary. Regardless of the various titles these schools utilize, they all prepare students for professional Christian ministry. In this way, the term *seminary* encompasses each of the different schools, and it is thus an apt phrase for describing graduate theological education in general.

Traditionally, a divinity school was affiliated with a denomination as well as a university, while a theological school was affiliated with a university but not a denomination. Today, however, divinity and theological schools are virtually synonymous.

Divinity or Theological School

One of the two most common names that seminaries sometimes employ—if not specifically utilizing the word *seminary*—is divinity or theological school. The distinctive feature of the divinity or theological school is its affiliation with a larger university. Essentially, all schools of divinity or theology are related to specific universities; most of these universities are Christian institutions. Yale University, for one example, is comprised of several professional colleges or schools. It has a law school, a business school, a medical school, a divinity school, and so forth. In this manner,

Yale Divinity School (www.yale.edu/divinity) is just one of several professional schools that constitute the university. Today, however, the term *divinity* is rarely used. Apart from what remains of the word in the titles of schools and degrees, the term *divinity* has generally been replaced by another word: *theology*.

This term, *theology*, denotes the systematic ordering of the Christian faith. Almost every course at seminary will invariably be related in some form or another to theology. And because theology is altogether interested in issues of faith, it is a subject that is offered only at Christian institutions—and for our purposes, seminaries. An example of a seminary that uses the term *theological school* is Perkins School of Theology of Southern Methodist University (www.smu.edu/theology), located in Dallas. As was the case above with Yale Divinity School, Perkins School of Theology is simply one of several professional schools that constitute Southern Methodist University. Yale Divinity School and Perkins School of Theology are both seminaries.

Theological Seminary

The other common name that a seminary may call itself—apart from a divinity or theological school—is a theological seminary. The distinctive feature of a theological seminary is its independence from a university. In contrast to a school of divinity or theology, in other words, a theological seminary is freestanding or independent; it is not related to a university or college. In most every other way, however, it is synonymous.

Examples of freestanding or independent seminaries are Chicago Theological Seminary (www.ctschicago.edu); United Theological Seminary (www.united.edu) in Dayton, Ohio; Virginia Theological Seminary (www.vts.edu) in Alexandria; and Wesley Theological Seminary (www.wesleyseminary.edu) in Washington, D.C.

Why I Use *Seminary* for All Graduate Theological Education

To maintain some uniformity and add clarity to our discussion, I hereafter use the word *seminary* in reference to all graduate theological education. This is, after all, the most common way of describing the variety of graduate schools that train Christian leaders. I will use the more descriptive terms *divinity school* or *theological school* only when I contrast them with a theological seminary, that is, an independent or freestanding institution. Otherwise, the term *seminary* includes both divinity or theological schools, on the one hand, and theological seminaries, on the other.

Two Major Names for Seminaries at a Glance	
Divinity/Theological School	Seminary affiliated with a university
Theological Seminary	Independent seminary; not affiliated with a university

School of Religion as Distinct from *Seminary*

In contrast to divinity and theological schools, on the one hand, and theological seminaries, on the other, there is a name that certain institutions go by that is sometimes confused with seminaries: schools of religion. The distinctive feature of the school of religion is its training of students for careers related expressly to teaching and research. However, schools of religion do *not* prepare students for the Christian ministry. For this reason, they are *not* synonymous with seminaries. Many graduate schools of religion are not even related to Christian institutions at all. They are one of perhaps dozens of other graduate departments offered under the auspices of a graduate school within a larger university. In this sense, graduate schools of religion are dedicated principally to academic endeavors or disciplines, and not practical ones—even at Christian schools.

Schools of Religion

- Prepare individuals for careers in teaching and research
- Distinct from divinity/theological schools and theological seminaries
- Exist within larger universities
- Are not considered in this book, because they are not seminaries

Let us consider an example from Boston University, originally a Methodist institution. At the graduate level, Boston University maintains two distinct schools for those interested in studying Christianity: the Religion Department in the Graduate School of Arts and Sciences, and the School of Theology (www.bu.edu/sth). Although both the department and the school offer the study of Christianity, they provide different services. Students who endeavor to study Christianity as a religion, that is, as a historical and cultural phenomenon (much as one would study history or literature), pursue a program in the Department of Religion. However, students who are pursuing professional Christian ministry enter the School of Theology at Boston University, the name of its seminary. Because schools of religion or departments of religion are not related to seminaries, we will not discuss them further in this book.

Seminaries are considered professional schools because they prepare students for a particular profession.

Seminary as Professional School

Now that we have a better understanding of the different names of seminary, let us discuss the particular structure of seminary education. As we do so, we will learn that seminaries operate in a similar way to other graduate schools in North America. Like medical schools, for instance, seminaries are considered professional schools because they prepare students for a particular profession—traditionally a profession in one of the following: pastoral ministry or the priesthood, theological education or teaching, missions or evangelism, administration, and so forth. Professional schools are both academic and practical.

Because seminary is a professional school, seminary curriculum is roughly divided into what could be called both theoretical and practical courses. However, each school and program has a particular area of expertise that will determine whether you receive more theoretical or more practical exposure. Seminary is, in this way, similar to other professional schools. During medical school, for example, students spend the majority of their first two years researching and memorizing facts about anatomy, physiology, biology, and diseases. This phase in their training is mostly theoretical. The next phase of training is more practical. For the remaining two years, students are trained in the hospital, where they work with patients suffering from real medical conditions—

> **Examples of Theory and Practice in Seminary**
>
> *Theory*
> - Memorizing biblical facts and interpreting biblical passages
> - Writing research and exegetical papers
> - Understanding the flow of church history and the nature of theology
>
> *Practice*
> - Counseling and consoling people
> - Officiating at weddings, funerals, and other church services
> - Becoming a more effective preacher and worship leader

although they do continue their research and reading during this process. Both the theoretical and the practical components are fundamental to professional development, but each school varies with regard to emphasis.

Seminary operates in a similar way. It incorporates both theoretical and practical components into its curriculum. Students therefore simultaneously study, for instance, important dates and events in church history (theory) as well as how to counsel grieving parishioners (practice).

Seminaries and Law Schools

Seminaries are also like law schools—another type of professional school. Like a law school, for example, a seminary does not require any particular major in your undergraduate degree. You could major in anything from

English literature (read any Shakespeare lately?) to botany. What they do require is that you have a bachelor's degree. This is because they are considered (post)graduate schools, as opposed to undergraduate schools (as colleges are).

Seminaries are similar to other professional schools such as law schools and medical schools. Most of what you will learn is how to research, write, and interpret important documents common to each field.

Both law schools and seminaries follow similar curricular models. Their typical degrees (the juris doctor and the master of divinity, respectively) entail roughly three years of full-time coursework. Most of what you will learn is how to research, write, and interpret important documents common to each field. These schools are designed to introduce you to the proper terminology needed to function successfully in that discipline. Although as professional schools they are supposed to be divided into theoretical and practical components, many professional schools tend to focus on the theoretical. The practical components emerge during your first years of work after graduation, or perhaps alongside your studies. Upon graduation, law school students traditionally studied for the dreaded bar examination, while many seminary graduates sought ordination from their particular denominations.

Financial Difference between Seminary and Other Professional Schools

Although a seminary is technically both a graduate school and a professional school, it is very different from, say, medical school or law school in one extremely important way. The years of training you receive in seminary will not materialize into . . . well, material things. In other words, you will not become wealthy just because you received one or even two degrees from seminary. You can virtually be assured that upon graduating from law school—even if you decide not to take the bar—you will get a higher-paying job than you had before you entered law school. Not so with seminary. While the story of Rick Warren—internationally known Christian author, pastor, and speaker—attests to the fact, for instance, that some seminary graduates have earned millions upon graduation, the degree of difference financially between a college graduate and a seminary graduate typically is not going to be substantial. In fact, the seminary graduate often makes less. The ministry is definitely a rewarding vocation, but it is not a lucrative profession. Whereas many students are attracted to law school or medical school in part because lawyers and doctors typically do well financially, the same is not true when it comes to seminary and those in the ministry.

Still Interested in Seminary?

Before you give up your dreams of going to seminary, however, let me back up a moment. Going to seminary is a wonderful experience, and very few people actually think they are going to become rich as a result of receiving a theological education. But I also think that it is fair for you to know beforehand what to expect upon graduation. As with everything else in life, your (financial) success depends on many factors. It depends on the seminary you attend, the occupation you pursue upon graduating, and the area of the world in which you choose to live. There are many more factors to consider as well. And it is the purpose of this book to help you come to terms with these sorts of issues. Attending seminary has been one of the most rewarding experiences of my life, and I intend to help you understand the nature of seminary education and how you can prepare for this wonderful endeavor as well. In the next chapter we will explore whether or not seminary is right for you.

*Seminary is one of the only professional schools in North America that will **not** increase your salary upon graduation.*

3

Discovering Whether Seminary Is Right for You

How I Found Myself in Seminary

I've always lived two separate lives. On the one hand, I've always wanted to live abroad. My first experience outside of the country was during high school, when I spent the summer in Brazil. I knew from that moment that I wanted to live in a different country, or at least to be very active in the international community. For that reason, I majored in Spanish during college. On the other hand, I'd always wanted to be a lawyer and a politician. For that reason, I also majored in political science.

Throughout my college days, I vacillated between being a linguist or a lawyer. Should I move abroad and start a language school? Or should I attend law school in the United States? I was at a crossroads in my life. So, as graduation day approached, I did what many people do: I delayed. I delayed the decision by attempting both. I looked into programs abroad, and I filled out applications for law school in America. I was caught between the two and unsure how to act when, all of the sudden, I believed that I was being pulled in a different direction: I felt compelled to enter seminary instead.

Knowing Whether or Not to Go

Although I was a little confused by this sudden turn of events, deep down I felt that going to seminary was the right thing for me to do. And as the years have gone by, I am thankful that I went. In this chapter you will learn that seminary is right for some people and not right for others. How do you know if it is right for you? You picked up this book for a reason. In fact, this book probably came your way because you have been thinking about seminary. If that is the case, perhaps you should enter seminary.

> **Are You Sure You Want to Go to Seminary?**
>
> - Seminary is time-consuming. A full-time student typically takes three to four classes per semester. The assignments in these classes include research papers, tests, quizzes, and presentations.
> - Seminary is expensive. A typical degree may cost between $25,000 and $50,000.
> - Seminary is not necessarily easy. It is after all *graduate* school. Be prepared for a challenge.

At the same time, however, you should not become a pilot just because you have perfect vision and would like to have some cool stripes on your sleeves. There has to be more to it. I hope, for instance, you do not think that you should attend seminary just because you are a devout Christian who wants to know more about God. If that describes your situation, understand that there are plenty of ways that you can meet this need without having to go to seminary. Seminary is a large investment, both financially and spiritually. It should not be entered lightly. However, seminary does serve a purpose and prepares you for full-time ministry—if that is what you want to do. In this chapter I will do my best to help you figure out if the cost is worth your while.

Look Who Is Famous and Rich without Going to Seminary

Seminary is not for everyone. There are many successful and famous Christian ministers who never spent a day in seminary. The excellent preacher and best-selling author Joel Osteen, for instance, is the pastor of perhaps the largest church in America—Lakewood Church in Houston— but he never attended seminary. Equally noteworthy is that Bill Hybels, one of the other most successful American pastors and Christian authors—at Willow Creek Community Church outside of Chicago—did not graduate from seminary (though he did receive an honorary doctorate from seminary). Finally, Brian McLaren, founding pastor of Cedar Ridge Community Church in the Washington-Baltimore area, and author of several recent books on contemporary Christian issues, never went to seminary. Are you beginning to detect a pattern?

Many successful Christian ministers never spent a day in seminary.

There are many other cases of influential Christian professionals who succeeded without receiving a theological education. This does not mean, however, that seminary is a waste of time. These Christians are exceptions, not the norm. They are like billionaire Bill Gates, who never graduated from college. Obviously, the typical college dropout does not go on to become one of the wealthiest businessmen in the world. Nor do most non-seminary graduates become internationally acclaimed Christian pastors, teachers, and writers. That certain individuals have succeeded without the "standard" education does not mean that you can do the same. Christianity is naturally stronger than any piece of paper or formal education, but you should not plan on skipping seminary just because others have done well without it. Actually, many of the more famous Christian preachers and teachers in North America have attended seminaries. They were trained well in theology, and their good training is what enabled them to become such effective leaders and ministers.

> **Do I wish I had attended seminary? Not for a minute . . . seminary . . . is too often a system of certification, not education.**
> *Brian McLaren*

What Do You Miss by Not Going to Seminary?

If I never go to seminary, you may be thinking, *what will I miss?* That is a good question, especially if you are in a situation that doesn't easily allow you to attend seminary. Technically, you could learn most of what seminaries teach by reading numerous books and working at a church or somewhere similar for a couple of years. Such an experience would give you both the theoretical and the practical components that are constitutive of seminary education. To tell the truth, this is the approach of many Christian workers all around the globe who do not have the opportunity to attend seminary.

This leads us to perhaps the most important question in this book: How do you know whether you should attend seminary or whether you should just get a job at a church instead? How do you know if you are ready to go to seminary? As I mentioned above, this is a decision that you must come to personally and communally. You must come to it personally by reflecting on

Questions to Ask When Thinking about Going to Seminary

- Do I believe that I have been called to go to seminary?
- Have I been in prayer about this, and does my congregation confirm it?
- Does my immediate family (my spouse or children) support this decision?
- Am I at a point professionally where I can dedicate several years to school?
- Am I able to finance a seminary education?
- Do I have the right personality, temperament, and interests to go to seminary?

your individual interests, abilities, and vocational objectives. And you must discern this communally as your pastor or priest, elders, and Christian friends pray with you and counsel you as regards this decision. You should additionally have the support of your immediate family (if you are married and have children).

The Jeff Foxworthy School of Theology

In this section we will take a test administered by the Jeff Foxworthy School of Theology. Aside from the occasional Yankee, we have probably all heard of Jeff Foxworthy and his characteristic refrain, "You might be a redneck if . . ." In good (Southern) Christian fashion, I am going to convert Foxworthy's saying into church parlance: "You might be a seminarian if . . ." If any of these correlate with your professional objectives, it is a good indication that you are a prime candidate for seminary.

You Might Be a Seminarian If . . .

- You want to be a pastor or priest (in any capacity).
- You keep arguing with people about theology and how church should be.
- You want to be a Christian counselor, therapist, or psychologist.
- You want to be a primary or secondary teacher (at a Christian school).
- You want to be a college or seminary professor (usually at a Christian school).
- You want to be a preacher or Christian speaker.
- You want to be a missionary or church planter (domestic or international).
- You want to be a theologically informed layperson, elder, or deacon.
- You want to be involved in Christian music or worship (in any capacity).
- You want to be a Bible translator.
- You want to be a chaplain.
- You want to be an administrator (in a Christian institution or organization).
- You want to be a Christian author.

· You believe you are led, but do not know exactly why (that was my story).

Checking Your Results

So how did you do? Did any of these professions or aims resonate with you? Are you ready to pack up your bags and leave tomorrow for seminary? *All right,* you may be thinking, *I am pretty sure by now that seminary is the right place for me. But how do I know when I am ready? How do I begin? And do I have to be ready to drop all my responsibilities right now?* Don't worry, I get it. You still have more questions and are not sure about this seminary thing. That's natural. You *should* be careful. It is a very big decision. Do not let anyone rush you into going until you and your community of faith believe that you are ready. Below we will continue to evaluate your compatibility with seminary by taking yet another exam (you might as well get used to taking tests now!).

Seminary Myth-Busters

Now we are going to look at another compatibility test of sorts. Have you ever heard of the television show *MythBusters*? It is a program by two commonsensical scientists who assess so-called myths to evaluate whether they are true. In the experiment below, we will test a few myths of our own. These are potential pitfalls when it comes to seminary. We are going to bust these myths once and for all. Think through them carefully.

1. To go to seminary, I have to have a bachelor's degree in Bible or religion.

Not so. Most seminaries admit anyone with a bachelor's degree. Although seminaries do not necessarily require a certain college major, they generally prefer students who have taken several courses in the liberal arts. In other words, they prefer students who have studied literature, history, philosophy, logic, and languages. This is because these courses are believed to better prepare you for the types of subjects that you will study in seminary.

What if you have never even taken a class in literature? That is not a problem; it will not keep you out of seminary. When all is said and done, seminaries admit students from every undergraduate field available, from anthropology to zoology. My advice is that in college you should study what you love learning about and what you do well. Following this advice may get you a degree in anything from engineering to German. You would most likely get more mileage out of your German degree while attending seminary, but a degree in engineering would always provide you with a back-up job if necessary. I personally know many students who have majored in engineering and have later done very well in seminary.

2. To go to seminary, I need years of ministry experience.

Not so. Remember that seminaries exist in order to prepare you for ministry. It is not a prerequisite for entrance. You do not go to medical school, after all, because you know how to perform an appendectomy: *they* are supposed to teach you how to do that. However, seminaries will expect that you have had some involvement in the Christian community. This involvement need not be extensive, but they would like to see some kind of experience on your part—whether as a Sunday school teacher, a youth leader, a summer camp counselor, or something similar.

Seminaries prefer students who have studied the liberal arts, but they admit students of every academic background.

If you are not already involved in a local congregation, I would encourage you to become involved as soon as possible. It would help you tremendously to spend a couple of months in ministry in some capacity before going to seminary. This activity need not be full time; the important thing is that you get some experience. You may even find out within a week that you are not cut out for such a career.

3. To go to seminary, I have to take the GRE (Graduate Record Examination, the graduate school equivalent of the SAT).

Not so. Few seminaries require the GRE. That is necessary only if there is a deficiency in your undergraduate studies or if you are applying for a doctoral (graduate) degree. As long as your grades aren't horrible, and you have decent recommendations, you should be in the clear. There are occasional exceptions to this rule, however. The University of Notre Dame Department of Theology (http://theology.nd.edu), in Indiana, for instance, typically requires most incoming students to take the GRE before being admitted. The reason is twofold. First, this school offers generous scholarships to incoming students, and the process is thus extremely competitive. Second, the

Seminaries do not typically require students to take standardized testing (at least for basic degrees).

University of Notre Dame is very well respected academically for theological studies; as such, it attracts very bright students.

4. To go to seminary, I have to first enter the workplace.

Not so. A seminary will not reject your application as a result of little or no work experience. Seminaries would certainly be enthusiastic if they observed that you have had past career experience, but you should not get a job after college just to improve your application. Understand that all schools thrive on diversity. This means that seminaries admit students of all different backgrounds and personal histories: students directly out of college, students who have worked for twenty years, domestic students, foreign students, and students who have traditionally been overlooked or neglected by theological education. Do you have a great opportunity to work for a couple of years before going to seminary? Then do so. Are you ready and financially able to go to attend seminary now? If so, enter seminary and gain experience along the way.

5. Seminarians have to attend classes full time.

Not so. Practically every seminary offers students the flexibility to attend school either part time or full time. It is up to you. Many schools these days participate in distance learning, or they offer classes at nontraditional times. Some classes are held one day a week, on the weekend, in the evening, or during the summer, as well as partially or fully online. Biblical Theological Seminary (www.biblical.edu), located outside of Philadelphia, offers degrees for people who work full time that can be earned in two or three years. Students take their classes in the evening and on the weekend, and fulfill many course requirements online. Many schools these days additionally offer classes via DVD or similar media. As a result, it is relatively easy to find a seminary that you could attend on a part-time basis or in a nontraditional format.

More and more students attend seminary on a part-time basis.

Of course, you can always attend school full time, or part time for a while and then full time. Just bear in mind that the longer you stay in school, the longer it will take to graduate. But by no means rush things for that sake alone. Life is a marathon, not a sprint. Are you supporting a spouse and kids? Do you have a mortgage? Are you bankrupt? If you answered affirmatively to any of these questions, you probably should attend school part time so that you can work either part time or full time as well. By contrast, are you without debt? Are you single? Are you ready to start your career? Then go to school full time. Find a job in the summer or on a part-time basis. Or better yet, do not work at all.

6. To go to seminary, I have to know exactly what I am going to do upon graduation.

Not so. You definitely do not need to know what you are going to do after seminary—only that you are called to go to seminary. Remember that most of us did not go to college completely sure of what we wanted to study or do for the rest of our lives. And of those who did know this, they probably changed their minds. You can go to seminary without knowing whether you want to be a teacher, a pastor, an administrator, or a layperson. In addition to the different programs and classes that you will take, both seminary faculty/staff and fellow students can help you discern what you are called to do upon graduation.

Nevertheless, it would naturally be helpful to have a good indication before you enter so as to save money, time, and frustration. I went to seminary not knowing exactly what I would end up doing. Would I be a missionary, a pastor, a teacher, or none of the above? What mattered most was that I believed that I was supposed to go to seminary. The rest fell into place while I was there. If that describes your situation, go to seminary. While in school, you will get a better feel for your interests and abilities.

7. I have to be a pastor or priest upon graduation.

Not so. The general makeup of seminaries today has evolved considerably over the years: from ones historically made up of future pastors and priests to ones currently full of students who are pursuing a variety of diverse career paths. Although seminaries will always be filled with future pastors, other, more nontraditional, opportunities abound. You can be an educated layperson, teacher, musician, writer, counselor, missionary, administrator, or professional basketball player (all right, not exactly—but you get the point). When I graduated from seminary, I got a job teaching Spanish to high school students. It never occurred to me that I would end up doing that after seminary, but life is full of surprises.

The trend today is for many seminarians to be in pursuit of professions outside of pastoral ministry.

I personally know of graduates who have entered fields very different from what they had imagined—including medicine, business, art, the military, and so forth. There is no set path.

Obviously, if you want to be a pastor, seminary is the place for you. But if you don't want to be a pastor at all—like most all of my friends from seminary, quite frankly—then you will actually fit in more than you think. One of my good friends entered seminary believing that he would be a pastor upon graduation. He is currently working full time at an art gallery. The trend today is for many seminarians to be in pursuit of professions outside of pastoral ministry.

8. I have to finance seminary myself.

Not so. There are many ways to keep money from coming out of your own wallet to pay for seminary. There are scholarships, denominational monies, local church support, grants, loans, assistantships, and part-time jobs that could defray the cost of seminary education. However, do not rely on this support as if it is already in the bank.

Research your school of choice, and be sure not to enter into seminary with an extremely heavy debt. The costs of seminary, like everything else in the world, are on the rise and definitely not cheap. One class, for instance, might cost you anywhere from $1,000 to $1,500. You have to be especially sensible financially when in graduate school, because most people will have already accumulated a certain amount of debt while in college. For this reason, many students work full time for a couple of years before seminary. That way one has less debt after seminary. (In the seventh chapter we will discuss in depth how you may be able to finance your education.)

9. In seminary I will have to write a dissertation.

Not so. Dissertations are usually reserved for more academic and advanced degrees. The run-of-the-mill seminary degree, the master of divinity, rarely requires a written dissertation or thesis. If you are interested in writing a dissertation or thesis while in seminary, then you should probably take a more academic route in your studies. This is a viable alternative for those who want a seminary education but do not want to become ordained pastors or priests. But only the advanced or purely academic degrees at a typical seminary will require a dissertation—not the standard degree.

10. To attend seminary, I have to live on campus.

Not so. Seminaries are, by design, graduate institutions. Practically speaking, this means that their students are adults and thus are not able to drop everything—their spouses, children, houses, cars, pets—in pursuit of a degree. In contrast to many undergraduate institutions, therefore, graduate schools do not require students to live on campus during their studies. Students live wherever it is convenient for them to reside.

Nevertheless, many seminaries do have a limited number of residential apartments. If you are willing and able to reside in them, there are many bonuses: they foster community; they are usually cheaper than houses and apartments in the surrounding area; they are within walking distance to class and the library; and they will enable you to make lifelong friends. However, each seminary is different. Some campuses offer no housing; some offer excellent accommodations for both singles and families; others have housing only for singles.

My general advice would be to live on campus if you are able. There are two sides to this: (1) Your seminary education does not have much value without the vibrant community you experience along the way. The friends you make at school are just as important as the classes you take. (2) Your primary obligation is to your spouse and children (if you are married or have children, that is). Remember that your family is probably sacrificing a great deal so that you can go to seminary; therefore, be very considerate of those sacrifices.

Although sometimes it is impossible, I recommend that students live near or even on campus.

I have lived on the campus of only one of the seminaries I attended, because the housing at the other seminaries was not conducive to my family's needs. But it was a great experience living on campus. In fact, there is usually a high demand for living on campus, and housing is frequently limited. As a result, you will need to contact the housing department at your seminary of choice and complete a form in order to be considered. Upon acceptance into seminary, the question of whether to consider campus housing should be at the top of your priority list.

Putting It All Together

Well, did we bust any myths? I thought so. There are many aspects that you need to consider when looking into seminary. In fact, there is one thing that you must always tell yourself: the more accurate knowledge I have about seminary, the better off I am going to be. It is not my intention that just anybody goes to seminary. My intention is to give you the best information possible and helpful guidelines so that you can base your decision on factual information. Seminary requires a great deal of time, money, and effort. Make sure that you know what you are getting yourself into. You will do well to discern this—as I discussed above—by prayer, discussion with your community of faith, research, and conversation with friends and family who will have your best interests in mind. I recommend that you reflect on this chapter, and begin to think about your compatibility with seminary. Do you believe that you are called to attend seminary? Are you ready to attend now? In the next section, we will discuss what you need to think about before attending seminary.

THINGS TO CONSIDER
BEFORE SEMINARY

4

Theological Affiliations, Traditions, and Denominations

My first year at seminary was very rewarding, but it was also quite challenging because the particular theological affiliation of the school differed considerably from my own and that of my home church. Several people warned me of this, but I responded that I was ready for a challenge. Although I am very thankful for the experience—as it taught me much about seminary and life in general—I was probably quite naive. Theological affiliation is extremely important when it comes to deciding which school to attend.

Theological affiliation is one of the most important factors to think about when deciding on a specific seminary to attend.

The next five chapters will address issues and topics that you need to consider before attending seminary. The specific topics will range from the size of the school you want to attend, to living on or off campus, to financing your education, to finding a seminary's proximity to a good coffee shop. As you read through these chapters, carefully note your preferences and other decisions that you will have to make. These will guide you when you customize your seminary of choice in a future chapter.

Theological Affiliation

Because of the experiences I mentioned above during my first year of seminary, the issue of theological affiliation became crucial as I thought about transferring to another seminary for my second year. In fact, this was for me perhaps the most important factor when I began looking into other seminaries. This was important to me not only because of my personal experiences, but also because I had heard of many other students who had attended seminaries that differed from them theologically. While at school the students became frustrated and were generally unhappy with their seminary experience. I did not want to end up like that, so I began searching only for those seminaries that reflected more closely the theology of the types of churches that I had attended.

Each seminary differs theologically and has a unique history that determines where it falls on the theological radar.

Eventually I found several seminaries that reflected my theological background. I also discovered through my research that each seminary has a unique history that determines where it falls on the theological spectrum. In this chapter, therefore, I would like to mention a select number of theological traditions. Obviously, there are many different types of institutions and theological traditions—far too many to mention—but below is a good sample. I have tried to organize the different theological traditions only in general terms. Be sure to speak with your community of faith, however, for more specific theological information.

Theological Traditions within Christianity

Among the hundreds of seminaries in North America, theological differences have been evident since the church's conception in the first century, and these divisions have naturally widened over the centuries—each new decade bringing with it new developments. Despite the differences in the way Christians construe their faith, however, almost all of Christianity can be divided into one of three groups: (1) Roman Catholic; (2) Orthodox; or (3) Protestant.

Within this division are three distinct forms of Christian expression and practice that have broadened over the years but which nonetheless converge in the essential doctrinal matters: belief in God, the significance of Jesus's death and resurrection, and the Spirit's guidance over the church. That is to say, although these traditions differ with regard to questions of worship—what is sometimes referred to as the liturgy—or what doctrines deserve more emphasis than others, each of these divisions is representative of the catholicity, or universality, of Christianity. In this section we will briefly discuss each of the three divisions, with an eye to how they relate to theological education.

Christianity
Catholicism   Orthodoxy   Protestantism

Roman Catholic Seminaries

The Catholic tradition is in many ways the original tradition of the Christian church. Traditional Christians before and after the legalization of Christianity in the first half of the fourth century were known as Catholics. Over the years the Catholic church developed a strong sense of tradition that stabilized its doctrines and practices. Specific emphases in the Catholic tradition are doctrines and practices related to Jesus's passion (his suffering on the cross); the importance of Jesus's mother, Mary; the role of earlier saints in the life of the church; and the belief that Jesus's body is specially present in the Eucharist or Lord's Supper and that his body actually changes into bread and wine—a doctrine called transubstantiation. In the sixteenth century the Catholic church became referred to as the Roman Catholic Church.

If you are Catholic and want to attend seminary, the best place for you to begin is your local parish.

There are many excellent Catholic seminaries in North America. If you are Catholic and want to attend seminary, the best place for you to begin is your local parish. There your priest will be able to help you through the process of selecting an appropriate seminary. It is even possible that your congregation has a tradition of sending its ministerial candidates to certain seminaries. This is, after all, a common way for some churches to train their local leaders. Speak and pray with your priest or local diocese for specific instructions about seminary education.

If you are Protestant (or Orthodox) and want to attend a Catholic seminary, it is probably best that you do so in a graduate degree program (for instance, a PhD) as opposed to a first degree, such as a master's degree (but more about degrees in chapters 13 and 14). Personally, I would recommend that Protestants get their first degrees from Protestant seminaries, and Catholics get their first degrees from Catholic seminaries (and Orthodox students from Orthodox seminaries). It is important for you to get to know your own tradition before you learn about another. Moreover, some seminaries require their students (at least for the standard seminary degrees) to be of the same tradition, by and large, of the school. If you already have a first degree from a seminary, then by all means try to attend a different seminary for a graduate degree if you desire. It would be a very educational and enriching experience for you.

Examples of Catholic seminaries are Aquinas Institute of Theology (www. ai.edu) in St. Louis; St. Augustine's Seminary (www.staugustines.on.ca) of Toronto, a participant in the Toronto School of Theology; St. Charles Borromeo Seminary (www.scs.edu) in Philadelphia; St. Mary's Seminary (www.stmarys.edu) in Baltimore; and Washington Theological Union (www. wtu.edu) in Washington, D.C.

Orthodox Seminaries

The term "orthodox" should not be confused with the lowercase term *orthodox*, which means "right thinking" in Greek. The Orthodox church formally separated from the Catholic church in AD 1054, and it has been largely influential in Eastern Europe (e.g., Greece, Russia, and the Ukraine). There are not many Orthodox seminaries in North America (about 2 percent of seminaries in the United States and Canada accredited by ATS are Orthodox—fewer than five in total [www.ats.edu]).

The Orthodox church shares the essential doctrines of Christianity with both the Catholic and Protestant churches, such as belief in God the Father, Son, and Holy Spirit; the divinity and humanity of Jesus, the Son; Jesus's resurrection from the dead; and the sacraments of baptism and the Eucharist. They differ from the two other branches of Christianity in their emphasis on the following: paradox and mystery; church tradition; how humans become more godlike or divine through faith in Jesus (*theosis*); and on the significance and solemnity of the liturgy.

The Orthodox church is probably the least represented of Christian traditions in North America.

Examples of Orthodox seminaries are Holy Cross Greek Orthodox School of Theology (www.hchc.edu) in Brookline, Massachusetts; St. Vladimir's Theological Seminary (www.svots.edu) in New York; and St. Tikhon's Orthodox Theological Seminary (www.stots.edu) in South Canaan, Pennsylvania.

Protestant Seminaries

Undoubtedly the most widespread tradition of seminaries in North America is the Protestant tradition. The reason is historical. Protestants played a significant role in the formation of the United States not only during the colonial period but, more importantly, subsequent to the formation of the American nation. After the Civil War, Protestant seminaries multiplied exponentially. In fact, Protestantism—as history would have it—is divisive, and there are literally thousands of denominations under its theological umbrella. We Protestants are like the broomsticks in *Fantasia*—the Disney movie in which Mickey Mouse experienced such consternation as he unsuccessfully attempted to limit the amount of brooms that were generated from the splinters on the floor. We just keep splitting apart and multiplying!

Generally speaking, there are two broad traditions of Protestants in North America: mainline and evangelical.

Below are just two different species of Protestants: the mainline and evangelical traditions. In a word, mainline seminaries are regarded as more liberal, whereas evangelical institutions are regarded as more conservative. However, because the words *liberal* and *conservative* mean different things to different people, I will use the more descriptive terms *mainline* and *evangelical* when referring to the two classes of Protestant churches and seminaries. These distinctions, however, are by no means airtight. Many Protestants fall somewhere in between or perhaps outside these two categories. I have been involved with both mainline and evangelical churches and seminaries over the years. The following descriptions stem from personal experience as well as study. The descriptions are not exhaustive but are simply used to provide a very general understanding of the diversity of the Protestant tradition.

MAINLINE

Mainline churches—and thereby mainline seminaries—constitute a cluster of theological denominations whose theology would be classified as moderate to liberal. Mainline churches tend to correlate their faith with contemporary culture more than do conservative Christians. They have a more pluralistic understanding of religion, which means that they are more willing to see the value and efficacy of other formal religions than conservatives are.

Mainline churches are usually very concerned about justice and racism. They believe in the complete equality of the sexes, often ordain women to the ministry along with men, and are highly involved in other social issues. Mainline churches also affirm the traditional doctrines of the church, such as the Trinity; however, they do not necessarily mandate belief in other ancient doctrines, such as Jesus's virgin birth. There are several denominations that comprise what are called mainline churches, including, for instance, the American Baptist Churches (USA), the Episcopal Church, the Evangelical Lutheran

Mainline churches are moderate to liberal theologically.

Church in America (ELCA), the Presbyterian Church (USA), the United Church of Christ (UCC), and the United Methodist Church (UMC).

Examples of mainline seminaries are Eden Theological Seminary (www. eden.edu) in St. Louis; Iliff School of Theology (www.iliff.edu) in Denver; General Theological Seminary (www.gts.edu) in New York City; Pittsburgh Theological Seminary (www.pts.edu); San Francisco Theological Seminary (www.sfts.edu); Trinity Lutheran Seminary (www.trinitylutheranseminary. edu) in Columbus, Ohio; and the University of the South School of Theology (http://theology.sewanee.edu) in Sewanee, Tennessee.

EVANGELICAL

Evangelicals come in many varieties. They tend to be more countercultural than their mainline counterparts, although many are certainly involved in contemporary culture. Evangelicals affirm the authority and, frequently, the infallibility of scripture. They also believe in the divinity of Jesus, his atonement of sin, and his bodily resurrection (remember to consult Appendix 3 when you come across unfamiliar theological terms). Evangelicals desire to evangelize the world, so that everyone can experience personal conversion. Many denominations are considered evangelical, but a few examples are the Christian and Missionary Alliance (CMA), the Evangelical Free Church of America (EFCA), the Presbyterian Church in America (PCA), and the Southern Baptist Convention (SBC). Many other evangelical institutions or seminaries, however, are interdenominational; thus, they are not connected to any particular denomination.

Evangelical churches are moderate to conservative theologically.

Examples of evangelical seminaries affiliated with denominations are Alliance Theological Seminary (www.alliance.edu) outside of New York City; Asbury Theological Seminary (www.asburyseminary.edu) in Kentucky; Trinity Evangelical Divinity School (www.tiu.edu/divinity) outside of Chicago; Harding University Graduate School of Religion (www.hugsr. edu) in Memphis; and the Evangelical School of Theology (www.evangelical.edu) in Pennsylvania.

What Is a Denomination?

In this chapter I have been integrating the word *denomination* more and more into our conversation. I have wanted to discuss the term in more detail, but I believed it was necessary to explain the term in relation to the different Christian traditions, particularly in relation to the Protestant tradition. In effect, a denomination is a specific religious association or division of Christianity, often within Protestantism—but not exclusively. There are literally thousands of denominations, ranging in size from millions of members to hundreds. Denominations can vary a great deal theologically, but all usually agree on the most important features of Christianity. However, it is not our purpose in this book to discuss each denomination. Instead, our task is to make you aware of them and to learn how your denomination may be of assistance when attending seminary.

A denomination is a specific religious association within Christianity that has its own organization and distinctive traditions.

Many churches and seminaries are officially connected to a larger denomination. Churches that are organized in this way share the same doctrinal beliefs—though there may be minor differences as a result of geography, culture, and emphasis. Not all churches and seminaries, however, operate under the auspices of a denomination. Many seminaries support no particular denomination. They are usually a conglomeration of multiple denominations, without advocating one over the other; they are variously called "interdenominational," "multidenominational," or "nondenominational."

Denominationally Affiliated

For the most part, it would be safe to say that your church has a counterpart in the seminary world. That is to say, if you happen to attend a church associated with the Presbyterian Church in America (PCA)—an evangelical denomination—there is good reason to believe that there is at least one seminary associated with that denomination somewhere in North America. Thus, if you are in good standing with that denomination, it is logical that you would seek a seminary where it maintains a school. This probably means, however, that you will have to move—but you have probably learned by now that seminary often entails sacrifice. In the case of PCA seminaries, there happen to be two seminaries affiliated with that denomination in North America: Covenant Theological Seminary (www.covenantseminary.edu) in St. Louis; and Knox Theological Seminary (www.knoxseminary.edu) in Fort Lauderdale, Florida.

Many seminaries in North America are affiliated with specific denominations.

Take an example from a different denomination. I have a friend who happens to be a lifelong member of the Christian Church (Disciples of Christ), a mainline denomination. Because his father is ordained in that denomination, and because he wanted to graduate from seminary without accumulating too much debt (the children of ordained ministers often have reduced tuition at institutions related to the denomination of their parents), he enrolled in a seminary sponsored by the Disciples of Christ. This denomination operates seminaries mostly in the southeast and central part of the United States. My friend's options were fourfold: Brite Divinity School of Texas Christian University (www.brite.tcu.edu) in Fort Worth, Texas; Phillips Theological Seminary (www.ptstulsa.edu) in Tulsa; Lexington Theological Seminary (www.lextheo.edu) in Kentucky; and Christian Theological Seminary (www.cts.edu) in Indianapolis. Obviously, each of the schools was equally appropriate according to his educational and theological criteria, but they may not have been optimal choices if he wanted to live in, say, California. The positive feature is that he can graduate with little or no debt, and he will be surrounded by likeminded people while in seminary. These are the types of situations that people will find themselves in when choosing a seminary that is affiliated with their current denomination. They will have to decide whether location, size, diversity, or theological emphasis is more important.

Advantages of Attending a Seminary of Your Denomination

There are several advantages to attending a seminary that is affiliated with your church denomination. Aside from having a better probability of receiving financial assistance when you are a member of a particular denomination, you usually have a better chance of admittance into the school. This is because seminaries, like other secular organizations, often prefer students who reflect their particular theology and ideals. What's more, if you go to a seminary of your denomination, there is a greater likelihood of your making lifelong friends. Your friendship with colleagues associated with your denomination will most likely continue because you will probably see them on a regular basis during denominational conferences, local church meetings, or other activities. These colleagues will be great support throughout your ministry. Whatever you have heard about ministry, know that it is tough. Sometimes it is like a desert. At times you may feel like you are all alone, just trying to stay alive and not be attacked by wild animals. At such times—and they will come to everyone at least once—having a close friend in a similar situation and of a similar theological background will prove to be priceless.

A possible detriment of attending a seminary in your denomination is that you will not be as exposed to different traditions.

Denominational seminaries serve other purposes besides facilitating friendship. A good way to know where a seminary lies theologically, for instance, is to see whether it is affiliated with a denomination; the theology of the denomination will largely determine the theology of the school. However, one of the possible weaknesses of attending a school whose denominational affiliation is your own is that you will not be exposed as regularly to other viewpoints. This could be its greatest detriment. But it is also important to keep in mind that every school has pluses and minuses. You'll have to decide on what those pluses or minuses are for you.

How to Find the Right Denomination

Although many students are members of particular denominations before they attend seminary, there are still other students who either are not part of any denomination or at least do not intend to become ordained in that denomination upon graduation from seminary. One reason may be that the student moved to an area where his or her original denomination is not represented. I know of others who left their earlier denominations in search for a new one as a result of their theological views changing while in seminary. As a result, I'd like to explain how to locate and evaluate a specific denomination. We'll do so in four steps.

The denomination of a particular seminary largely determines the theological emphasis of that school.

Four Steps to Follow toward Finding a Denomination

1. Make a list of several churches around your area by searching online, consulting a telephone book, speaking with friends, or driving around your town.
2. Over the next few weeks, visit some of the churches. Then narrow the search to one or two of the churches, and attend it regularly.
3. Speak with the leaders of that church, and discuss with them your aspirations, training, and potential for ministry.
4. Locate a seminary that is affiliated with that denomination, or at least find a seminary that the denomination has some form of (informal) relationship with.

Attending a Denominational Seminary Different from Your Own

There is another important component to denominational seminaries. What if there is a really good denominational seminary that you are interested in, but it happens to be of a different denomination than your own?

Is that going to be a problem? Most likely it will not. Many seminaries allow students of other denominations to attend without joining that denomination. I have taken classes at three denominational seminaries over the years, while being a member of just one of them. I learned a great deal about other theological perspectives, and it challenged me to become more thoughtful with regard to my own theological positions. Because other students did not presuppose what I did, I was forced to thoughtfully consider—for the first time really—the viewpoints of others. This experience added greatly to my theological formation, but it is certainly not for everyone.

I have a friend who spent his entire life in the Lutheran tradition. He had attended a church in the ELCA (Evangelical Lutheran Church in America) denomination since birth, and he had even graduated from a college aligned with that denomination. When it came time for him to attend seminary, he decided to attend a Presbyterian school. Why? Because he felt like he needed to see things from a different perspective for a while before ultimately being ordained by his denomination as a Lutheran pastor. Years later he is very glad that he decided to do this.

Examples of denominational seminaries are Claremont School of Theology (www.cst.edu) in southern California, a school affiliated with the United Methodist Church; Lutheran Theological Seminary (www.ltsp.edu) in Philadelphia, aligned with the Evangelical Lutheran Church in America; and New Brunswick Theological Seminary (www.nbts.edu) in New Jersey, part of the Reformed Church in America.

Positives and Negatives of Attending Your Denominational Seminary

Positives	Negatives
Easier admittance	Less innovation or novelty
Better chance of scholarships	May have to move (out of state)
More in common with students	Less diversity

Nondenominational, Multidenominational, Interdenominational

Although a plethora of seminaries are related to denominations, there are still many others that are unaffiliated. This does not mean, however, that they are theologically neutral. In fact, there is no such thing as a neutral seminary. Every seminary exists for a specific reason and teaches within some particular theological tradition. Although they may not have an *explicit* relationship with a denomination, they will usually have unwritten relationships with many different denominations or other traditions. In other words, every seminary has a particular community of faith that it caters to. Find out the community, and you will be able to figure out if that school is right for you.

Some people attend seminaries that are different from their own tradition in order to see things differently; others prefer to attend their denomination's seminaries.

Seminaries Not Affiliated with Denominations

- Nondenominational: not affiliated with any denomination
- Multidenominational or interdenominational: includes multiple denominations
- Apart from these specific distinctions, these terms all refer to the fact that a seminary does not endorse one denomination over another

Finding a Nondenominational or Multidenominational Seminary's Constituency

When a seminary is not directly related to a denomination, it may be difficult to determine where it lies theologically. However, this does not mean that it is simply neutral as regards theological issues. It is not. As discussed above, it just does not have an official relationship with a particular denomination. When this is the case, there is a way to discern the seminary's community or constituency.

Steps to Follow toward Understanding a Seminary's Community of Faith

1. Find the seminary's website. Search for something that says "About the Seminary" or "History of the Seminary." Alternatively, check "Doctrinal Statements" or "Beliefs." This will clarify things.
2. Find out the names of the schools the faculty attended and try to discern their denominational affiliation. The professors are typically the best indicator of the makeup of the school. Oftentimes seminary websites will contain a brief biography of each professor, which will highlight what type of church (or denomination) the faculty member attends.
3. Call or e-mail someone in the admissions office to find out where most seminarians end up upon graduation. If any became pastors after

graduating, ask which denominations they belong to or what other organizations they joined.

Finalizing Theological Traditions and Denominations

No seminary is neutral. Each one is related in some way to a tradition.

As you may have figured out in this chapter, the different theological traditions and denominations represented in North America are no less apparent in seminary than in the church at large. We began this new section by discussing how theology impacts seminary, but theological affiliation is just one consideration when it comes to thinking about seminary. In the next chapter, we will discuss several more factors such as the size and location of the school you want to attend.

5

The Outside of Seminary

In the previous chapter we discussed theological traditions, an important component to seminary that you will need to think about before enrolling in classes. In this chapter we mention several other components. While we do so, I encourage you to take the time to think carefully through these issues. They are certainly not fundamental to being successful in seminary. However, the more time you take now to decide on these issues, the better off you will be once in seminary. Think of this chapter as an attempt to customize your school choice to your personality. To continue the analogy with cars, these considerations have less to do with which type of car you drive and more to do with your decision of an automatic versus a manual transmission, an SUV versus a sports car, or a red car with a sunroof versus a black car with a hardtop. Though not essential, they are still important considerations.

This chapter is an attempt to fit your school choice to your personality.

1. University-Based Divinity/Theological School or Independent Seminary?

This chapter is dedicated to components outside or around the physical seminary. For this reason, we will begin our discussion by noting some

All seminaries fall into one of two categories: (1) those within a larger university and (2) those that are independent.

of the differences between the two overarching types of seminaries. As we noted in a previous chapter, for instance, all seminaries fall into one of two categories: those within a university (usually called schools of divinity or theology) and those that are independent (usually called theological seminaries). There are no differences academically or professionally between the two. They both prepare students for Christian ministry. They only really differ in how they are organized institutionally. I have attended both and I have found that each has unique characteristics.

University-Based Seminaries (Divinity or Theological Schools)

Naturally, the most distinctive feature of a divinity or theological school is its relation to a larger university setting. As a result of this relationship, there are usually more opportunities and resources available at these schools than at independent seminaries. This is because seminaries affiliated with universities often have larger libraries, more general activities, guest speakers, and greater resources.

Seminaries within universities often have greater resources and offer more activities than independent seminaries.

The first seminary that I attended was a divinity school. I appreciated attending this type of seminary first, because I was right out of college and—since it was part of a larger university—being around so many younger people wasn't unfamiliar. Perhaps you are right out of college. If this is the case, it is possible that you too may feel more comfortable in a university setting than at an independent seminary with students who may be older and who may even be married or have children. Attending a seminary that shares affinities with college life would be more logical for you at this point in your education. At the same time, however, I do not want to imply that seminaries within universities are for younger or single students only. This is far from the truth. When all is said and done, both seminaries within universities and those without have students of all ages and all circumstances.

Examples of divinity and theological schools within universities are Beeson Divinity School of Samford University (www.beesondivinity.com) in Birmingham; Talbot School of Theology of Biola University (www.talbot.edu) in Los Angeles; and the University of Chicago Divinity School (http://divinity.uchicago.edu). None of these schools is formally affiliated with any particular denomination.

Attending a Divinity or Theological School within a University

Upside	Downside
Larger and more extensive libraries	Too much like college life (you have already spent years at college)
Food options galore (cafeterias, restaurants, college hangouts)	More politics (the politics of the university can interfere with the seminary)
Exercise facilities (gyms, tracks, fields, courts, and other facilities)	Too hectic and busy
Sports (football, soccer, tennis, basketball, baseball)	
Other intellectual activities, organizations, and events (college speakers)	
Greater diversity	

Independent (Freestanding) Seminaries

The second type of seminary is the independent or freestanding seminary. This kind of seminary is related neither to a larger university nor usually to any other institution. It is made up solely of seminarians. The freestanding seminary is different from the divinity or theological school only in its independence from all other schools.

After my first year of attending a divinity school, I got married, and my wife and I moved to a different part of the country. This is how I ended up attending an independent seminary. Although I had enjoyed being part of a seminary within a university, I found attending an independent seminary friendlier and more like a family. One of the reasons for this, perhaps, is that many seminarians who attend independent schools are facing the same issues that you are, and they will therefore provide a great sense of camaraderie and encouragement during your seminary days. Independent seminaries additionally tend to have more opportunities for spouses or children (if you have them) to make friends, and it always seemed to me that independent schools had more students with families. In this sense, independent seminaries perhaps have a more close-knit feel to them than divinity schools.

I have noticed that independent seminaries have a very close-knit feel to them. They are like a family.

Three examples of independent seminaries are the Atlantic School of Theology (http://astheology.ns.ca), in Nova Scotia, Dallas Theological Seminary (www.dts.edu), and Memphis Theological Seminary (www.memphisseminary.edu). Because they are each interdenominational seminaries, they are not officially affiliated with any particular denomination.

Attending Independent Seminaries

Upside	Downside
Better chance (perhaps) to build community and relationships	Fewer resources (library, money, faculty)
Everyone has more in common with one another (values and ambitions).	Fewer activities (sports, events, organizations)
The students are sometimes more mature and focused.	Isolation (from different viewpoints)
Usually more freedom and less (university) politics	Less known (sometimes) than a university-based seminary

2. Size of School?

"Will that be a Venti or a Grande decaf cappuccino, sir?" Hey, it has worked for Starbucks, one of the world's most successful coffee chains, so why not seminary? Do you want to go to one of the largest seminaries on the planet (Fuller Seminary [www.fuller.edu] in southern California, for instance, has around 4,000 students), or a much a smaller school? Whether you realize it or not, the size of the school you choose is extremely important. Naturally, larger and smaller seminaries each have their positives and negatives. What is important is that you feel comfortable with the size of the school you attend.

Larger Seminaries

I still remember driving through the impressive campus of Southwestern Baptist Theological Seminary (www.swbts.edu) in Fort Worth, Texas. It was wonderful, because the campus was essentially a small city! I know many people who prefer attending larger schools because they have more resources at their disposal: larger libraries, more professors, more money, more classes, more programs, and usually more opportunities. Some students also prefer larger seminaries because they can meet new people every week.

Examples abound of larger seminaries in North America—of all different theological traditions. However, I have noticed that the largest of these seem to have two characteristics: conservativism (evangelical) and independence. Examples of such schools are Southern Baptist Theological Seminary (www.sbts.edu) in Louisville and Gordon-Conwell Theological Seminary (www.gts.edu) north of Boston. Two examples of larger divinity schools within more mainline universities, however, are Perkins School of

Theology of Southern Methodist University (www.smu.edu/theology), in Dallas, and Brite Divinity School of Texas Christian University (www.brite.tcu.edu), in Fort Worth. An example of a larger Catholic seminary is the Catholic University of America School of Theology and Religious Studies in (www.religiousstudies.cua.edu), in Washington, D.C.

Smaller Seminaries

Smaller seminaries have their own appeal. They are quieter, usually friendlier—even familial—and they may also allow for relationships to grow faster than at larger seminaries. I actually prefer smaller schools over larger seminaries for these very reasons. When I was thinking many years ago about colleges to attend, I deliberately chose a school that was not very large. This mind-set tended to guide my decisions when it came to seminary as well. Although there are positive features that students may miss by attending a smaller school, many students still prefer smaller seminaries, because they like to get to know the students in their classes and the professors who teach them. Moreover, because many people feel uncomfortable in very large classroom settings, a smaller school can be less intimidating.

The Skinny on Larger Seminaries

Positives	Negatives
Better resources and reputation	Less teacher interaction
More financial assistance	More impersonal
More (innovative) programs	More businesslike
Better technology	May be more competitive
Greater diversity	Harder to distinguish yourself from others
More contacts and friends	You may get lost when trying to find the bathroom!
More opportunities	
Better course / program selection	

The Skinny on Smaller Seminaries

Positives	Negatives
More teacher interaction	Less class selection
Individualized attention	Less diversity
Closeknit community	Fewer networking options
You will not have to valet-park!	Fewer resources

3. Location?

What is it they say in the world of business and real estate? "Location, location, location!" Things are no different in the world of seminary education. For many people, location is one of the most important factors—sometimes *the* most important factor—when choosing a seminary. Many students have children, mortgages, family, lifelong friends, and so forth. Therefore, it is not easy for them to uproot their lives and the lives of their families for seminary. Anyone who is married or has children should seriously consider the difficulties of moving and location as of chief importance when deciding on seminary.

This does not mean, however, that you should attend the seminary next door just because it is very close to your house. Finding the right seminary is like finding the right wedding dress or the right car. When looking to buy a new car, for instance, you don't just buy the first car you see that is the closest to home. Instead, you research to find the most reliable, most comfortable, and most economical car. Afterward, you go and test-drive it. You want to see if it feels as comfortable as it looks and to observe whether it drives as well as you envisioned. If it works out as you imagined, you discuss options (financial and otherwise) with your salesperson. You want to confirm that your monthly payment is reasonable and that your investment is worth the financial sacrifice that you will have to make. Finally, once all the negotiations have been settled, you buy the car. The same is true with seminary. You want to make sure that your seminary of choice is going to be perfect for you, which means that you may or may not have to move to find it. Whatever the case, be sure to factor in the importance of location when deciding which seminary you should attend.

Think of finding the right seminary as finding the right car. You do not choose the first one you see; you choose the best one for your circumstances.

Attending Seminary in the City or in the Country

Apart from physical distance, there is another aspect of location that you will need to think about when considering seminary: do you want to attend a more urban or a more suburban school? In other words, do you want to live in the city or the country? There is a great degree of difference between the two. This is because the location of a seminary actually determines the structure and even the theology of the school.

Naturally, the closer a seminary is to the city, the more it will look like a city; and the closer a seminary is to the suburbs, the more it will look like suburbia. Take your pick. Have you lived in the city your entire life? Are you comfortable in that environment? Then it may make the most sense to attend a seminary in the city. Or maybe the opposite is true for you? Maybe you are looking for something different? Either way, it is important to understand that both urban and suburban seminaries offer positive and negative features. One is not inherently better than the other; it has more to do with preference, comfort, and even your future career objectives. Some programs, for instance, offer concentrations and even degrees in urban studies. Thus, if you are interested in such a program, you will probably not want to attend seminary in the country! Here are some things to consider when it comes to the characteristics of urban and suburban seminaries.

You might attend a more urban or suburban seminary based on to your aims upon graduation. Do you want to become a country pastor or a social worker in the city?

Characteristics of Urban and Suburban Seminaries

Urban	Suburban
Better grasp of social issues	Usually more commuters
Faster pace and tempo	Slower pace and tempo
Less parking	Adequate parking
Potentially more crime	Often safer
More diversity	Less diversity (mirrors the makeup of the neighborhood)
Usually offers concentrations in urban studies	Wealthier (sometimes)

Pulling It Together

So which type of seminary resonated better with you? I have actually attended both urban and suburban seminaries. Both were instructive. I personally felt more comfortable at the suburban seminaries—but that is only because I was raised in a small town in East Texas! The seminary I attended in the city, however, was very enriching and allowed me to see things in a different way. What I appreciated more than anything was the diversity of people as well as the cultural awareness of issues that many suburban seminaries do not emphasize as much.

Questions about Location

• Am I willing to move for seminary?
• Am I willing to move out of state?
• How can I prepare for relocating?
• How will moving affect my family?

Two examples of urban seminaries in the north are Mc-Cormick Theological Seminary (www.mccormick.edu) in Chicago, and Union Theological Seminary (www.utsnyc.edu) in New York City, an affiliate of Columbia University. Examples of suburban seminaries are Ashland Theological Seminary (www.ashland.edu/seminary) in Ohio; and Reformed Episcopal Seminary (www.reseminary.edu) outside of Philadelphia.

Attending a Seminary via Distance Education

Another issue of where to attend seminary is an increasingly popular option, distance education and online learning. As I will discuss later, more and more seminaries are offering programs through distance education. Students do not have to relocate to attend seminary, because most classes are conducted online and through mail. A distance learner still interacts with students and professors, but mostly through the Internet and, perhaps, group phone calls. All seminaries accredited by ATS, however, are required to have a certain percentage of classroom instruction conducted on campus.

The intervals for such classes are very short: usually a week or two at a time. Thus, students need not move; in fact, many schools that offer these programs even provide low-rent dormitories or apartments, or they will at least help you make appropriate housing arrangements for your short-term campus requirements and visits. The number of on-campus class requirements varies from program to program and school to school, but each school strives to make this process smooth and painless.

This form of education is ideal for more second-career students who are simply too established in their lives to relocate for seminary. If you are in your forties or fifties, are married with children, own your home, and do not want to move, this is probably your best option (unless of course there happens to be a good seminary close to your area). If you are single or in a position to relocate, it is probably best to enroll in a more traditional program at seminary.

There are several seminaries these days that offer programs via distance education. In fact, more and more seminaries will probably begin offering such programs. The following are just a few of the ever-increasing number of seminaries that offer programs via distance education: Concordia Seminary (www.csl.edu) in St. Louis;

Hartford Seminary (www.hartsem.edu) in Connecticut; North Park Theological Seminary (www.northpark.edu/sem) in Chicago; and Wartburg Theological Seminary (www.wartburgseminary.edu) in Dubuque, Iowa.

4. Living on Campus or off Campus

Another factor when considering seminary has to do with deciding whether to live on or off campus. This important decision must be made immediately upon deciding on a school. As I have stated before, every student who attends seminary will have a unique set of circumstances. Some students will come to seminary single and right out of college; others will be married with children and a mortgage; and still others will have different circumstances. As a result, you will have to make the best decision based on your own situation. Although your circumstances may not allow it—and if so, that is perfectly fine—I recommend that students attempt to live on campus, or at least very close by.

> **Questions to Consider with Distance Education or Online Learning**
>
> • Am I in need of a seminary education without relocating?
> • Am I able to motivate myself and do my work independently?
> • Do I have a computer with Internet access?
> • Am I able to take off work for the occasional short-term course at seminary?
> • What will I miss by not enrolling in a more traditional, on-campus program?
> • Do my family and church support my decision to attend seminary this way?

Living on Campus

I recommend living near the campus because I believe that your seminary experience should be more than just your coursework. And living near or on campus will allow for greater relationships to form and for more learning to take place. You need to always remind yourself that you do not attend school just for the degree. It is, rather, about the community and the experience you have of debating ideas with friends and professors; about your classroom conversations spilling over to the cafeteria; and about having to share living quarters with your roommates! Living at the school will allow you to make lifelong friends and become more involved in the community. By the time you graduate, the friends you have made will last a lifetime, and they will have made your classes and education more worthwhile. Years after seminary, you may not remember what you studied in a particular class, but you will remember the friends you made outside of that class.

Years after seminary you may not remember what you studied in a particular class, but you will remember the friends you made outside of that class.

On the more practical side, it is usually cheaper to live on campus than elsewhere. Campus housing is typically less expensive than other types of housing in the area, such as rental houses or apartment complexes. (And how many graduate students do you know who have extra money to spend?) What is more, depending upon what type of campus housing is available at your seminary of choice, your school housing may even be better than other types of housing. Whether or not your seminary actually has better housing conditions, it will—I should hope!—have more friendly and more trustworthy neighbors.

Living off Campus

I understand that certain students or families are simply unable to live on or near campus. I also understand that not all seminaries provide adequate housing. Each school differs: some are unable to offer any residential living; some offer it just for singles; others have many apartments that can accommodate large families. (Gordon-Conwell Theological Seminary [www.gts.edu], outside of Boston, for example, has many excellent apartments for families.) If you are not able or simply do not want to live on campus, it is likely that you will have to work a little harder than others at getting involved in seminary. But do whatever is best for your family and your own circumstances.

Positives and Negatives of Living on Campus

Positives	Negatives
More community	Space is limited
Shorter commute	Longer commute to work (perhaps)
Cheaper housing	May miss friends and family
Christian neighbors	Insularity (all are like you)

Factoring in the Factors

In this chapter we have looked at several factors when it comes to seminary. None of these factors is crucial when attending a seminary, but I do believe that they can change the nature of your seminary experience. The more you know about seminary before attending, the happier I think you will be once you are there. For this reason, in the next chapter we will continue talking about more considerations when looking into seminary. In the meantime, you may want to ask yourself the following questions.

Factor Chapter Checklist

___ Should I attend a university-affiliated seminary or an independent one?

___ Should I attend a larger or smaller seminary?

___ Should I move (perhaps even out of state) or stay local?

___ Should I attend a seminary in the city or the suburbs?

___ Should I live on campus or off campus?

6

The Inside of Seminary

From the Outside to the Inside

The last chapter concentrated on things that you need to think about with regard to the residential aspects of seminary. This chapter will move from the outside to the inside of seminary by focusing on issues related more to its internal operations. We will begin with the issue of accreditation and end with a discussion of the specific mission or general specialization of any given seminary. Although this chapter discusses topics that are perhaps less tangible

This chapter moves inside seminary, focusing on issues related to the internal operations of seminary.

than the former, they are worth thinking about. These topics are, in fact, at the center of every seminary, and they determine the quality of education provided.

1. Accreditation

Since the twentieth century, many schools have sought accreditation. This means that they meet certain objective criteria set by a governing agency in regard to educational integrity. It also means that these schools seek accountability in relation to other institutions. The most notable seminary accrediting agency in North America is the Association of Theological Schools (ATS), which was founded in 1918 but only began accrediting seminaries in 1938. However, there are many other accrediting agencies as well—whether at the national or the regional level. Currently, there are more than 250 seminaries in North America accredited by ATS. This institution represents a membership organization of professionals all across North America; it supervises accreditation, standardizes curriculum, publishes its findings, and generally guarantees professional and academic integrity. Although some schools do not seek accreditation—for one reason or another—all the schools mentioned in this book are accredited by ATS.

Whether Accreditation Is Necessary for Your Professional Objectives

Depending on what you do upon graduation, whether your seminary of choice is accredited is an important issue for you to consider. (However, you should know that many denominations require their prospective clergy to graduate from accredited seminaries.) I have heard people say, "I really like this seminary, but it is not accredited. Is that all right?" It depends. Do you want to teach at Harvard Divinity School or another estimable seminary one day? Then go to the accredited school! But if you do not want to teach, going to a school that is not accredited is not necessarily a bad thing. It all depends on your goals after graduation. Just be very, very careful. I once had a friend, for instance, who attended a nonaccredited school for a couple of years. Afterward she moved back home and wanted to transfer her two years of coursework to a local, accredited school. The school would not take her credits. She either had to start all over or never graduate!

This does not mean, however, that graduates from nonaccredited schools are professionally immobilized or unable to find good jobs upon graduation; many find great jobs. Just as discussed in an earlier chapter about certain individuals who have succeeded in professional ministry without earning a seminary degree, there are equally important and successful Christian ministers in North America—and all around the world, quite frankly—who have not received degrees from accredited seminaries. My advice on the matter is this: if you are able to attend a seminary accredited by ATS, do so. It cannot hurt to attend an accredited seminary, but it could hurt if you do not. What is more, by graduating from an accredited seminary you will have more opportunities, and you will never be barred from additional education—should that be necessary—or from a particular job because of a perceived deficiency in your education.

2. Faculty

The second factor that we will discuss in this chapter has to do with the faculty. The faculty is perhaps the single greatest influence on the school you attend and what you will learn when you attend it. A great faculty translates into a great school, whereas a mediocre or, worse, an inferior faculty translates into an inferior seminary. I know a pastor, for instance, who visited a seminary and decided to attend it on the spot as a result of a short discussion that he had with two of the professors there. He walked into their offices disappointed because the teachers that he wanted to talk to were not there that day. However, by the time he walked out of each of their offices an hour later—literally in tears and blown away by their spiritual warmth and passion—he called his wife on the phone and told her to pack their bags! Years after graduating from that seminary he still reminisces about how impressive the faculty was. The moral of the story: The professors at a particular school should be a major component to your decision about seminary.

The faculty is perhaps the single greatest influence on the school you attend and what you will learn when you attend it.

Meeting and Learning About the Faculty

Since the very beginning of education, students have flocked to this school or that one because of its teachers. It is the people after all—and not the buildings or whatever else—that make a school. What is more, it is the theology and the interests of the professors that dictate where the school lies theologically. In this sense, chances are that if you like such-and-such a professor, you will probably like the school as well.

Fortunately, there are excellent professors these days who have published widely enough for you to get a sense of their theological interests and affiliations. Moreover, with the continued advances of technology, you can easily locate any professor you would like to learn more about via the Internet. You need only search their name and then check out the website of the school where they teach. In fact, many professors have personal webpages or, at the least, a paragraph or two written about them at their respective

66 If you find yourself in seminary concern yourself not so much with what courses you take, but from whom you take them. 99

Tony Campolo (Christian author and scholar)

schools that states their interests and publications. Just look for a faculty directory at whichever school you are interested in and check out the professors there. If you see someone who looks interesting, shoot the professor an e-mail or even call him or her on the phone at school to talk about seminary. Do not be shy! Speaking with prospective students, after all, is part of the job description of professors.

The Importance of a Good and Considerate Faculty

I hate to break it to you, but even theological education is imperfect. Even at seminary you will not uncover the Christian faith in pure form, descended from heaven! You will be exposed instead to the perspectives of the faculty and be led to examine theology from a particular point of view. It is the faculty, after all, who determine what you read, what you hear, and ultimately what you learn. For this reason, it is important that you trust what is being taught and by whom it is being taught. Take into account, for instance, Jesus's advice in this respect: "You shall know [good faculty] by their fruits" (Matt. 7:20).

What to Look for in Faculty Members

Generally speaking, the faculty at any given seminary is usually very small and selective. Naturally, the number of faculty depends on the size of the school, but many seminaries may have only around ten or twelve faculty members. Consequently, it is necessary—from the perspective of a student—that the faculty be competent and professional. Unlike college, where you may have had dozens of different professors—so if you did not like one, you could just wait a semester and pick a different one!—in seminary you will probably have only a few teachers. The faculty will shape your theological development more than anyone else. It is crucial therefore that you trust this faculty. I understand, of course, that it is difficult to get a feel for a faculty member from a website, a publication, a brief meeting, or an e-mail. Getting to know someone takes a long time. But I suggest that you make an effort to do at least some research about a faculty member or two. It is important, and I believe that it will pay off in the long run.

The David Letterman School of Theology

You have probably heard of David Letterman's famous countdown on his late-night television program, but you may not have heard about the famous countdown of the most important attributes of seminary professors.

In case you missed that episode, I will rebroadcast it for you. Below are the ten most important qualities that faculty members should possess in order to qualify as your professors of choice at a particular seminary.

10. **Education**: They have doctorates, and from respectable schools.
9. **Experience**: They have practical experience. Do any of your professors teach classes on missions? Then make sure that he has actually been a missionary!
8. **Publications**: A strong faculty is one that publishes regularly— books, articles, and pamphlets. Be sure to read such materials if possible.
7. **Accessibility**: You can have the most brilliant professor in the world, but if she is never around when you need to speak, there is a problem.
6. **Ordination**: If a professor is ordained, which denomination was it with? Make sure you do not disagree strongly with that denomination!
5. **Diversity**: The more diverse the faculty is, the more thorough it will be. Look for differences in nationality, gender, education, and theological perspective.
4. **Camaraderie**: See how the faculty members treat one another. Do they frequently quarrel? Then watch out for that school!
3. **Friendly Face**: How does the faculty look? Of course, looks alone are not everything, but they do go a long way in revealing a personality.
2. **Hobbies**: Martin Luther said that a theologian who does not have a hobby is not a real theologian. That sounds about right.
1. **Humor**: A good sense of humor goes a long way. A theologian who does not laugh is probably not a very good theologian.

3. History/Mission

A component related to the faculty is the history and mission of each school. This is because all schools, historically and currently, exist for a particular reason. Each seminary has its own history and mission that determines its future. That history may be one hundred years old or it may be ten years old. Either way, each seminary was formed for a particular reason. Maybe it was founded in response to another seminary's change in policy with regard to certain doctrinal positions. Or maybe a group of individuals formed the school to emphasize something that other seminaries were not stressing.

Whatever the reason, the point is to realize that no school was ever founded because a couple of people were bored one day and wanted to have some students to boss around! Consequently, I recommend that you check out the history of your seminary of choice. You can do that either by logging onto the school's website and finding it there or by ordering its catalog. One of these sources will most likely contain information about the formation of the seminary.

The history of an institution determines its future. If, for instance, a seminary was founded thirty years ago to put more focus on the Bible than seminaries were doing at that time, you can be quite certain that this history will still be a major component of the seminary today. Consequently, if you disagree or are uncomfortable with the history of the seminary, then you will most likely not be a good fit at that school. Conversely, if you are in full agreement with why and how a seminary was formed, this is a good indication that you would fit in well there.

Westminster Theological Seminary (www.wts.edu) in Philadelphia, for instance, was founded in 1929 to counter what were perceived to be liberal tendencies at Princeton Theological Seminary due to a reorganization of the board and faculty. This history is still vital to the nature of Westminster, and it determines the school's functioning theologically—in the past as well as in the future. The historic doctrines of the Reformed faith play a very important role in the identity of the school.

Graduate Theological Union (www.gtu.edu) in Berkeley, California, by contrast, was founded in 1962 with the express purpose of uniting many of the disparate religious traditions and graduate institutions in the Berkeley area. Accordingly, students are able to take classes at various religious institutions and are in constant dialogue with not only Christians of all varieties, but also Jews, Buddhists, and Muslims. These two schools—Westminster Theological Seminary and Graduate Theological Union—offer excellent educational opportunities for students interested in seminary, but they differ widely in their theological commitments and professional objectives. Taking a few minutes to peruse the history of a particular school before attending it will help you decide whether the school is right for you; and, as in the case of these two schools, it will enable you to detect where the schools are heading in the future.

Discovering a Seminary's History

There are many ways to locate specific information about a seminary. For our purposes here, we will isolate just one way—a school's website.

Although we will discuss how to locate and navigate seminary websites more fully below (in the eighth chapter), I would like to briefly mention how you can get swift access to, say, a school's history or mission by way of the Internet. We will do this by examining one of the oldest seminaries in the country—Bangor Theological Seminary (www.bts.edu) in Maine—a mainline school affiliated with the United Church of Christ (UCC). The website at Bangor Theological Seminary is typical of seminary websites in North America, and it therefore serves as a fine model for this exercise.

Seminary History Exercise

1. Enter the BTS website (www.bts.edu).
2. Find and then click the link labeled "Prospective Students," which will direct you to more specific information about the school.
3. Now click the first link, labeled "About BTS."
4. This link will lead you to the information we wanted to view—a synopsis of the history and mission of the school, with additional links available for interested students.
5. Other seminary websites operate similarly. Take a few minutes now to locate one in your area, and look through it (for specific schools, enter the excellent website operated by ATS, which includes all seminaries accredited by that agency: www.ats.edu). Be sure to explore both the history of the school and any interesting links you come across. This is good practice, and you may discover the seminary of your dreams by doing so!

A School's Mission Statement

Another component to consider, in addition to the history, is the school's mission statement. Usually the history of the institution and its mission statement are consonant. If the mission or the history of the school differs considerably from your own personal history and educational objectives, then do not go to that school. Instead, find a school that excites you when you read its history and its mission. That is a good indication that you are headed for the right school.

One of the most direct ways to discover a seminary's distinctive theology is by reading its mission statement.

The mission statement at Mars Hill Graduate School (www.mhgs.edu), outside of Seattle, Washington, for example, is very specific. Intrinsic to the school's mission is the objective of

preparing leaders in the church who will be culturally and scripturally sensitive and savvy. The seminary strives to be innovative in the way it approaches
theological education, as well as in how it construes the nature of theology
to be relevant to the greater cultural environment in which it is situated.

Weston Jesuit School of Theology (www.wjst.edu), outside of Boston,
also maintains a very specific mission. This school was originally instituted
to provide philosophical training to prospective priests of the Society of
Jesus (SJ)—a religious order within the Roman Catholic Church. Over
the years, however, the mission has evolved. Although Weston Jesuit still
offers theological education to future ordained ministers of the Catholic
Church, the school also strives today to provide educational opportunities
for Christians with other professional objectives—including, for instance,
the objectives of laypersons. What is more, the school's affiliation and cooperation with other schools in the Boston area (via Boston Theological
Institute) is yet another important feature of the mission of Weston Jesuit
that allows for students to be exposed to several different theological traditions outside of the Catholic faith.

4. Specialization of School

Another factor to consider when searching for a seminary has to do with the
school's specific educational interests. Each seminary has a particular area in
which it does well. In the academic world, this is called "specialization." Some
seminaries are excellent at preparing students to become professors and scholars—such as Princeton Theological Seminary
(www.ptsem.edu) in New Jersey, a school well known for its
heritage of providing excellent educational opportunities for
students. Other schools are regarded for their expertise in
forming great missionaries. Columbia International University
Seminary and School of Missions (www.ciu.edu/seminary)
in South Carolina, for instance, produces missionaries each
year who travel the world as ministers of the gospel.

Every seminary has a particular area of ministry it does well. If possible, try to find a school that specializes in your area of interest.

Other schools excel in other areas. Fuller Theological
Seminary (www.fuller.edu) in Pasadena, California, for instance, maintains
an entire school dedicated to psychology and counseling. St. Mary's Seminary (www.stmarys.edu) in Baltimore, has a long tradition of educating
future priests. Finally, still other seminaries—such as Regent College (www.
regent-college.edu) in Vancouver, British Columbia—are known for providing holistic training that can be applied to any number of careers.

By providing examples of all of these different schools, however, I am not implying that they do poorly in other areas. Princeton Theological Seminary, for instance, attracts students of various professional interests, and not just academic ones. Students of all kinds attend schools of all kinds; however, some schools excel in one area over another. Hence, if you want to become a missionary, it just makes sense to find a seminary that specializes or does well in forming missionaries. In such a school you would find greater resources than you would at a school that specializes in pastoral ministry or academic subjects. Further, you would meet students with similar interests who would be of great support when looking for employment or an area of the world to minister to.

> **Finding a Seminary's Interests**
> 1. Check the school's website.
> 2. Ask people who might know.
> 3. Visit the campus.
> 4. E-mail or call the school.

So how do you know which seminaries specialize in what? That is the difficult part. Seminaries are very diverse. Every school has its share of future pastors, professors, missionaries, laypeople, musicians, and so on. No matter where you go, you will find students of all different backgrounds and interests. At the same time, though, each seminary has a particular focus or interest. The best way to figure out what that focus may be is to visit the campus or enter the seminary's website. If you do visit the campus, talk to the students, professors, and staff. Ask them what they think their seminary does best. Do they graduate more laypeople or professors? Are they more interested in academics or pastoral ministry? That is going to be your best indicator.

Howard University Divinity School (www.howard.edu/divinity) in Washington, D.C., for instance, specializes in the African American religious heritage and scholarship. One of its objectives is to empower its religious community and to prepare leaders who will serve the world by healing racial differences and by pursuing justice in ministry. Consequently, it makes sense that those who agree passionately with such a statement would do well to attend Howard versus another school. Other schools pursue other areas of interest.

Getting Ready for the Next Step

By this point you have probably realized that there are many things to consider when looking into seminary. With so much at stake, you may be thinking, *How in the world am I ever going to find a school that is right for me?*

Before we answer this question, however, we need to talk about a few more aspects of seminary. There are still many additional issues that we have not considered. For example, how much money does seminary cost? And how do I go about financing my education? In the next chapter we will address these questions.

7

Financing Your Seminary Education

Seminary and Money

Cuba Gooding, Jr. will be forever known in the world as a result of his catchy phrase in the movie *Jerry Maguire*: "Show me the money!" Like it or not, Hollywood has infiltrated more than just your local movie theater: It has infiltrated a seminary near you! "Show me the money" is unfortunately an apt phrase to describe the cost of seminary. As is the case with education in general, it takes money to go to school and eventually earn money. Even worse, perhaps, is that in the past several years most colleges have made large increases in their tuition, and I am sad to say that the same is happening at seminaries as well. What is more, because all seminaries require an undergraduate degree for admittance, many seminarians maintain debts of thousands of dollars from their college loans before ever entering seminary. However, there is good news for you. Although seminary prices increase each decade, there is more financial assistance available each decade as well. There are more scholarships, loans, grants, and other ways to finance your seminary education available today than ever before. In this respect, it is certainly a great time to attend seminary.

Seminary tuition, just like college tuition, is on the rise in North America. Be prepared to spend a lot of money!

The goal of this chapter is to discuss the financial aspects of seminary. In the previous three chapters, we have looked into several important components to seminary that you need to think about before your first day of class. The monetary aspect of seminary that we will discuss in this chapter is the concluding chapter dedicated to these issues. For many readers, financing your education will be a major component when deciding whether, when, and where to attend seminary.

Financial Aid Department

One of the good and bad aspects to most individual seminaries is that they maintain financial aid departments. This is very good in the sense that the entire department is dedicated to helping students locate and receive money for their seminary tuition. The department is usu-

Contact the financial aid department at your seminary of choice as soon as possible.

ally very effective and helpful, and you will want to get to know the people in the department during your first semester at school. However, the bad thing about schools having financial aid departments is that they are there for a reason: they exist only because seminary has become so expensive over the years and few people can pay for their education independently! Whatever the reason for their existence, though, I recommend that you get in touch with the financial aid department at your seminary of choice (or even consult the department at the college you attend if you are still in school). Speak with the department earlier than later.

Scholarships

The first area that we will discuss when it comes to financing your education has to do with scholarships. If you are smart, have good grades, and obtain great recommendations, you may qualify for a scholarship in seminary. The types vary from school to school. Some pay for all of your classes, while others pay only a little. (Even if you secure a scholarship, however, it is important to understand that you will still most likely have to pay for your books in addition to other miscellaneous items. This can get very pricey over the course of a few years.) Scholarships come in a variety of forms and sizes: scholastic, denominational, ethnic, geographic, type of degree, and so forth.

If you are interested in receiving a scholarship—and I would encourage you to at least consider it—the best plan of action is to contact each seminary you are interested in and ask for a booklet with the different types of available scholarships. Many seminaries maintain a comprehensive document that lists all of the various scholarships related to the school. Frequently such a list is attached to a seminary's annual catalog, so be sure to send an e-mail or make a phone call to your school of choice requesting a catalog.

Some seminaries will even list the types of scholarships they provide on their websites.

With regard to receiving scholarships, some are very specific: You must be a female student from New England who intends to be a foreign missionary. Other scholarships are less specific: you must be enrolled as a master of divinity student with at least a 3.0 grade-point average. One reason that there are so many different scholarships is that there are so many different people or organizations that sponsor them: alumni, businesses, families, schools, and other organizations.

Receiving a scholarship is an excellent way to finance your seminary education. Be sure to apply on time!

As you can imagine, scholarships are awarded quickly; the key is to apply very early and to make your application look as brilliant as possible. I remember visiting one seminary and paying a visit to the financial aid office while there. The person in charge answered all of my financial questions and even gave me a list of several pages that contained all of the scholarships available at that institution. On the form were at least one hundred options available for financing my education. Upon perusing the list, I discovered about a dozen scholarship possibilities.

When Applying for a Scholarship

- **Research, research, research**: Scholarships abound at schools, but many students fail to notice them for lack of appropriate research. Speak to a financial aid adviser very soon, look into any businesses or organizations that offer scholarships, research online, or find a book at the bookstore that discusses the topic.
- **Make deadlines**: The early bird gets the worm. No matter how brilliant you are, you will not receive a scholarship unless you apply on time. Some of the deadlines are early, so apply as quickly as possible.
- **Get practical experience**: Get as much school or work experience as possible before applying to seminary, especially in an area related to your field of interest. Demonstrate to your school of choice that you are qualified and experienced. Then highlight this experience when filling out the scholarship applications.
- **Do well academically**: Academic scholarships are not the only kind of scholarships that seminaries offer, but they are very common. The better you do academically during college or graduate school, the better opportunity you will have of securing an academic scholarship.
- **Fill out application materials well**: If you have excellent grades and a lot of experience but cannot write a coherent application essay, you will probably not receive a scholarship. We will talk about this aspect of seminary in the next chapter; for now, however, keep in mind the following: when it comes to the application process, be thorough, honest, specific, succinct, and creative. And find someone—someone responsible and smart!—to proofread and review your essays and other required materials.
- **Look for denominational support**: Discuss your plans of attending seminary with your local church denomination. Perhaps it can offer you a scholarship or another type of financial assistance. Denominations often provide excellent scholarships for those who qualify.

If you would like to get a seminary scholarship, your best option is to do as well as possible during college or graduate school and to fill your summers or other free time with real ministry experience. Do you want to be a missionary? Then go on a few mission trips. Do you want to lead worship? Then get involved with a choir or the worship team at your local church, or even look into starting a small band or group. Scholarships are difficult to obtain, but they are worth the effort—especially if you think you could qualify.

Loans

In addition to scholarships, there are several loans available to seminarians. Some are at good interest rates; others are not. When speaking of loans, it is important to consider whether you already have any debt from college or graduate school. Loans are double-edged swords: they are great at enabling you to pay for school, but in the long run you will pay for them. Just like scholarships, loans come in various shapes and sizes. Talk to the financial aid office at each seminary you are considering. It is the job of this department to acquaint you with your financial options. One last thing: be proactive about loans and money. Figure out your financial situation before even applying to seminary. The more you know before enrolling, the better you will be—and the less debt you will accumulate during seminary.

Steps to Getting Loans for Seminary

1. Speak directly with the financial aid office at your seminary (or current school if you are still in college or graduate school).
2. Apply for FAFSA (Free Application for Federal Student Aid) after January 1. This requires a good deal of time and information, so be patient. Then select the lender that offers the best rates—which could range from Bank of America to Nellie Mae.
3. Decide whether you want to be considered for subsidized loans (the government pays the interest while you are in school) or unsubsidized loans (your interest accrues while in school).
4. Consult your budget to see how much money you will need for each semester year—keeping in mind miscellaneous expenses (food, school supplies, and so on).
5. Verify with the financial aid office at your school whether the loan will be sent to your home address or to the seminary you will attend.
6. Examine your financial status annually, and do as much as possible to eliminate any debt (by working or cutting back on expenses). Always remind yourself that most Christian ministers are not rolling in money!

Grants and Work-Study

There are two alternatives to scholarships and loans that we haven't discussed. These are grants and other financial assistance that you could possibly receive by working at your school of choice.

- **Grants**: A grant is money received from a particular organization or institution. You do not have to pay it back—that's the best kind! Grants can be based on academics, ethnicity, geography, professional objectives, or other criteria. Consult your school for more specific information.
- **Work-Study**: Many institutions offer financial assistance to their students by providing them with jobs on campus. For instance, I have had friends at seminary who have mowed the school's lawn, cleaned toilets, stuffed envelopes, and researched for professors, to make money for school. Work-study is a great alternative to the secular workplace, because the school will be flexible with your schedule. You will either be paid directly, receive a tuition discount, or even receive free tuition on limited courses. Check with the human resources department at your institution of interest for more information.

Denominational Assistance

As I briefly noted above, another alternative to financing your seminary education independently is to consult your official denomination—if you are a member of a particular denomination, that is. Some denominations will gladly assist you in financing your seminary education. One of their jobs as an organization is to recruit future workers and leaders, and they sometimes designate a certain amount of money each year for students who want to attend seminary. If you do not qualify for tuition assistance, or if your denomination does not provide that kind of support, it could at least help you in other ways: internships for experience or remuneration, networking or connecting you to some other person or institution that can help, paying for your books or other living expenses while in seminary, and providing other resources. Whatever the exact result, talking with those who lead your denomination is a wise thing to do before going to seminary.

Many denominations maintain their own seminaries where they train future Christian leaders. Thus, if you are in good standing with your denomination and want to be around likeminded people, I recommend seeking out the financial opportunities that could arise from enrolling in a seminary

Attending a seminary of your denomination sometimes results in securing financial assistance.

supported by your denomination. I was very fortunate my first year, for instance, to attend a seminary from my childhood denomination. This particular school financed the greater part of every student's education. If I had not been part of that denomination and had not known some important individuals within it, I would not have received such generous financial assistance. Maybe your denomination provides something similar; if not, it should have other resources for helping you through seminary.

Support from Family, Friends, and the Local Church

I have been very blessed in my life to have the support of my parents. They paid for virtually all of my undergraduate education and helped me financially through seminary when needed. I could not have made it through school without them. Maybe someone in your family has it in his or her heart to help you through this time in your life. It is certainly worth thinking about: you never know what might result until you ask. Going to seminary to help make a better world with better people, after all, is a wonderful thing; maybe your friends or family will see your sacrifice and want to help you in that endeavor. Possibly you have some other acquaintances that could help? Perhaps some of your friends or family would consider offering a portion of their tithe each month toward your education.

Before you even think about attending seminary, speak with your local church. Perhaps it can help in financing your education.

You might also consider speaking with your local minister or church board. If anyone should help you through seminary, it should be your local church. Present your case to the elders or leaders in your church. Explain your vision for the future as well as your financial situation while you are in seminary. Perhaps they will surprise you with their generosity.

Paying for School through Working

"I made my family disappear." If you have ever seen the movie *Home Alone*, you know that sometimes we are left alone to deal with life. And it is a cold, hard fact that many seminarians pay for school out of their own wallets. Just like little Kevin in *Home Alone*, these seminarians are on their own—receiving no financial assistance from parents or other family members. If you are not able to get a scholarship or financial support from your church or family, you will most likely have to pay for school independently. This is certainly not the ideal situation, but sometimes it is the only situation. There are many ways that this can be done.

Paying for Seminary Independently

- You could work full time for a few years before seminary and save money.
- You could work part time and attend school full time or part time.
- You could work full time and attend school part time.
- Your spouse could work while you attend school.
- You could downsize by selling your car or house.
- You could work in the summer and winter to pay for classes in the fall and spring.

Whatever path you follow when it comes to paying for school, know your budget and consider your financial situation before you go to seminary. I have a friend, for example, who worked for a number of years before enrolling in seminary so that he would be able to finance his education as well as support his family in the process. He very wisely took into account how many years it would take him to sustain his family while in school and worked until he secured the sufficient means to stay ahead financially while in seminary.

Financial Adviser

Before we turn to the actual costs of seminary, I would like to mention one last financial alternative. Instead of looking for ways to receive money, maybe we should think about spending money. Have you ever heard of the adage "You have to spend money to earn money"? I know this advice may sound terribly foolish—particularly for those who, like me, did not have much money to begin with—but let me explain what I mean.

Perhaps you are like me and find the financial world difficult to understand. At times I compare my income with my expenses and wonder where all of my money goes! If this is the case for you, one option may be consulting a financial adviser. One of my good friends, for example, was recently admitted into seminary. The first thing that he and his wife did was to contact a financial planner. They did this so that their planner could help them understand their financial position as they enter this exciting, yet expensive, phase of their lives. Their decision to do so was wise. Financial planners are able to calculate your earnings and counsel you on how to spend your money in the most efficient way.

You may also want to sit down with a representative from your bank and discuss possible options there. The benefit of doing so is that your banker will understand your financial situation, and he or she should be able to provide sound financial counsel as regards your economic needs for the next few years. Even if you decide not to discuss your financial situation with a professional adviser, it is important that you be aware of where you are financially.

Cost of Seminary

In the previous section we talked about how to finance your education. We learned how to investigate loan options, how to get scholarships, and how to pursue other alternatives for paying for your seminary education. In this section we will discuss the actual costs of seminary by examining the typical price of classes, as well as miscellaneous expenses. We will continue with the topic of money for one very good reason: seminary is expensive! It is difficult to specify exactly how much seminary costs, because it depends on each school and each student's personal circumstances and needs. It also depends on which degree you pursue, what part of the country you live in, whether you have a job or a family, whether you have a scholarship or other financial assistance, whether you attend full time or part time, and whether you live on campus or some other place. But we will do our best to estimate. We will also take into consideration miscellaneous expenses for the average seminarian.

Price by Class and Program

Perhaps the simplest way to discuss the cost of seminary is by examining how much each individual unit or class and program costs. This is because most classes at each individual seminary charge the same amount of money (except for more advanced courses, which are more expensive). Many schools advertise their prices by unit or credit, each class typically comprising two to four units. Yet there is also another important cost difference: the price varies according to how many classes a student is required to take for his or her specific program.

Let us examine two very common and basic seminary degrees: the master of divinity and the master of arts (see chapters 13 and 14 for seminary degrees). The master of divinity, the classic seminary degree, consists of approximately thirty courses, whereas the master of arts, a very popular degree today, typically consists of around fifteen to twenty courses—though each program and school is different. To get a general idea of the price of seminary, we are going to examine the tuition of these two degrees at three different schools. These schools all differ geographically and theologically. Note that the following prices are for the 2006–2007 school year. The prices have been approximated and are not exact.

Examining Prices at Individual Seminaries

1. Talbot School of Theology of Biola University—Evangelical, interdenominational seminary outside Los Angeles (www.talbot.edu)

Master of Divinity

Per Unit	Required Units for Degree	Overall Cost
$396	96–98	$38,000

Master of Arts

Per Unit	Required Units for Degree	Overall Cost
$396	56–66	$24,000

2. Sacred Heart Major Seminary—Roman Catholic seminary in Detroit (www.aodonline.org/SHMS/SHMS.htm)

Master of Divinity

Per Unit	Required Units for Degree	Overall Cost
$398	110	$43,000

Master of Arts

Per Unit	Required Units for Degree	Overall Cost
$398	40	$16,000

3. Andover Newton Theological School—Mainline seminary outside Boston, affiliated with the American Baptist Church and the United Church of Christ (www.ants.edu)

Master of Divinity

Per Unit	Required Units for Degree	Overall Cost
$433	90	$39,000

Master of Arts

Per Unit	Required Units for Degree	Overall Cost
$433	48	$21,000

Miscellaneous Expenses

Besides the cost of your specific degree, it is also important to consider miscellaneous expenses when in seminary. These expenses vary greatly from person to person and place to place. However, as most everyone would agree, financial considerations are of the utmost importance for most seminarians. To state the obvious, it is burdensome to spend an additional $20,000 or $40,000 after your college education—especially for a profession that is not prosperous financially! For this reason, it is important to isolate how much money you will need to sustain yourself (and a family if you have one) while in seminary. As above, we will examine these expenses by using the information provided by a couple of different seminaries based on the 2006–2007 academic year. The expenses have been approximated.

Examining Miscellaneous Expenses at Individual Seminaries

1. Drew University Theological School—Mainline seminary in northern New Jersey, affiliated with the United Methodist Church (www.drew.edu/theo.aspx)

Item	Expense
General school fees	$1,000
Books and supplies	$1,000
Room and board	$11,000
Total Items for Three Years	**Total Expense**
$ 13,000 x 3 years	$39,000

2. Denver Seminary—Evangelical, interdenominational school in Colorado (www.denverseminary.edu)

Item	Expense
General school fees	$400
Books and supplies	$800
Room and board	$10,000
Total Items for Three Years	**Total Expense**
$11,000 x 3 years	$33,000

Totaling the Costs

As I stated above, these costs are approximate. It is not possible to state exactly how much money is needed for you to sustain yourself while in seminary. (You will certainly want to do your own research and calculating. These examples serve only as guidelines on getting started.) In fact, most of what we have learned in this chapter is that living in North America is costly—no matter where you live or what your profession is. Seminary simply adds to your normal expenses.

Seminary Expenses besides Tuition
• Books/supplies
• Food
• Housing
• Insurance
• Transportation
• Entertainment

The purpose of examining these different expenses has been to reinforce how important it is to consider your financial situation before you attend seminary. Seminary is certainly expensive, but so is living and eating regularly! Besides paying for tuition each semester, you will have expenses from books, food, housing, insurance, transportation, and entertainment. Over the years this can get very pricey, so prepare for these expenses. It is never too early to begin thinking about how to finance your education. Paying for school might possibly be the greatest obstacle when it comes to attending seminary, but do not give up hope. Think through this chapter carefully, and begin the process of pursuing financial assistance as early as possible.

Chapter Checklist

____ Consult the financial aid office at your seminary of interest soon.

____ Research diligently about money for school, using books and the Internet.

____ Pray and speak with your local church or denomination.

____ Investigate scholarships, loans, work-study, and so forth.

____ Talk with your family and friends about money for school.

____ Decide whether you will work in seminary, and plan your budget.

____ Think about miscellaneous expenses and how you will pay for them.

8

Steps toward Finding and Applying
to the Right Seminary

I began my first year of seminary the fall after graduating from college. I seriously considered just three seminaries: one in Texas, one in California, and one in New Jersey. In hindsight, I was naive. Although each of the three schools that I applied to was well respected and capable of delivering a solid education, none ultimately correlated with my personality and temperament, my geographic preference, or many of the other preferences that we have discussed in this book (if only I had read this book then!). However, by the time I began looking for a different seminary to attend for my second year, I had learned my lesson. Not only did I research many schools and programs to find the best fit for my circumstances and objectives, but I also did something else I had done at only one of the schools before my first year: I visited each of the different schools I had applied to, and I thought more about where I would best fit in.

The Goal of This Chapter

In this section we have discussed many features of seminary education that you will want to think about before attending seminary. We learned about many of the different theological traditions, the outside and inside of seminary, as well as the financial aspect of school. This chapter is the culmination of this section, because you will take all that you have learned in the previous chapters and apply them to your circumstances. We will determine which factors are most important to you when considering seminary, and then walk through the steps necessary to locate and apply to specific schools.

Making the Big Decisions about Seminary

Life is about decisions. Every morning that you wake up (or afternoon for you college students!), you are forced to make countless decisions: What should I wear today? What do I want for breakfast? What time do I want to leave for work or school? What radio station should I listen to? Seminary, just like life in general, is also about decisions. What type of school do I want to attend? Do I want to relocate or stay in the area? Should I enroll in this program or that one? How much money do I want to spend? Because there are so many decisions when it comes to seminary, it is necessary to have some way of deciding what is most important when trying to find the right one.

You need to decide which seminary to attend based on your specific circumstances and preferences.

To help you find out what is most important to you, we will customize your interests and preferences about seminary so that you can find the best school for your circumstances. As you go through the chapter, take the time to really think about what considerations are most important to you. Because everyone is different, every student will ultimately have different priorities. Nevertheless, everyone needs to go through the same process of deciding what they are, and then how he or she will make decisions based on those preferences.

In the chart below, I list many of the factors that we talked about in this section of the book. As you read through them again, decide which of them you believe to be most important in deciding what kind of school you want to attend. For each, you will have only two options, and they are mutually exclusive.

Factors When Deciding on a Seminary (List # 1)

Accreditation of school	Accredited by ATS	OR	Not accredited by ATS
Affiliation of school	Affiliated with denomination	OR	Not affiliated with denomination
Location of school	In state	OR	Out of state
Size of school	Larger	OR	Smaller
Type of school	University-based	OR	Independent

Type of program	Basic or first-professional	OR	Advanced or graduate
Type of degree	Master of . . .	OR	(Usually) Doctor of . . .
Educational model	Traditional (On Campus)	OR	Distance education

Locating Specific Seminaries

Probably the easiest and most direct way to locate a specific seminary is by entering the excellent website maintained by the Association of Theological Schools (ATS): www.ats.edu. ATS is an organization in North America that is committed to setting certain requirements for postgraduate theological education. The Association of Theological Schools—headquartered in Pittsburgh—is composed of staff members who are engaged in specific issues related to postgraduate theological education. Its Commission on Accrediting is responsible for accrediting and generally regulating its member seminaries. In this book I refer only to seminaries that are accredited by ATS; I will assume that you will attend only such a school.

The website maintained by ATS contains numerous resources that are potentially very helpful for those who are either contemplating seminary or are already in a program. For our purposes, however, we will concentrate on using this website only to locate specific seminaries of interest. On the website's main page, there should be several tabs that display what resources or information the association offers. Click the tab labeled "Member Schools." There you will be directed to the member schools of ATS. Bookmark this page on your computer. It offers three main ways to locate a seminary: alphabetically, denominationally, and geographically.

Check out the excellent website maintained by ATS at www.ats.edu. Every member school of ATS can be accessed on its webpage by alphabetical order, denominational or theological affiliation, or geography.

i. Theological or Denominational Affiliation and Geography

Now that we are in a better position to connect to actual seminaries, you will need to have your priority list available. The two factors that we will start with have to do with theological or denominational affiliation as well as location or geography. If theological or denominational affiliation is one of your priorities, you will want to begin your search for a seminary by clicking on the link labeled "Denominational Index of Member Schools." Upon doing so, you will be directed to every member school, organized according to denomination or theological affiliation—beginning with Canada and then moving down into the United States. Scroll down the page until you find the denomination or theological affiliation that best accords with your own. If, for instance, you happen to be a Baptist who lives in the United States, you will scroll down the page until you come across the designation "Baptist" subsumed under all the American seminaries. After finding all of the Baptist seminaries in the country, you will then need to find your specific denomination.

Once you find a particular seminary of interest and click on it, you will be directed to the data that ATS has compiled about that school: accrediting status, the president and vice president, location, theological affiliation, available degrees, student enrollment, and so forth. This represents the latest data about the seminary and thus serves as a brief yet instructive introduction to the school. If you like what you see about the school, click the link that takes you directly to the seminary, and explore its website more fully.

The second factor that we will consider in this section has to do with geography. Click on the link named "Geographic Index of Member Schools." Let us say, for instance, that you happen to live in California. And because everybody knows that California is the best state in the United States, you refuse to attend seminary elsewhere. As fortune would have it (or good sense would have it, according to you California natives), there happen to be many seminaries in California that you could possibly attend—of various theological positions. Just scroll down the page until you come across all the seminaries in that state; afterward, check out the schools that are closest to your city or area, or that look promising.

If you happen to live in a different part of the country, however, you may not be so fortunate as to have many seminaries in your area. Some states and certain Canadian provinces are not well represented; in fact, some areas do not have any seminaries. If you live in New Hampshire, for instance, you will have to relocate to attend seminary—or at least commute to a seminary somewhere in New England (or enroll in distance education). In larger states and cities, however, there is probably at least one seminary close by, maybe even several.

II. Size and Type of School

Besides affiliation and location, there are two other deciding factors: the size and type of the school. Size can make an enormous difference in your seminary experience, as we discussed in a previous chapter. Fortunately, there are many sizes of schools accredited by ATS, ranging from fewer than a hundred students to several thousand.

If you want to know how many students such-and-such a seminary has, you need only click the link of a particular school (already arranged—as noted above—according to alphabet, denomination, or geography). What constitutes a large or a small school is a subjective question, but generally speaking, I would say that a seminary with less than a hundred students is a small school while any seminary with more than three or four hundred students is a large one. In fact, most seminary enrolments fall somewhere in between these numbers, though some schools may have around fifty students, whereas others may have more than a thousand.

Generally speaking, a seminary with less than a hundred students is a smaller school while a seminary with more than four hundred students is a larger school.

There is one more thing about student enrollment that you should know. Although certain seminaries have more than one campus or school, they may display only the total number of students they enroll, not the populations of their individual campuses. Thus, the number of students you see displayed may not be the number of students you would see on a single campus on a normal basis; in fact, once you consider that many students either attend part time or are enrolled in different programs, you may not even see half that number of students on a regular basis while at school. For exact enrollment information, consult your school of interest.

Another factor in deciding on a seminary has to do with the type of school, that is, whether it is a university-based divinity/theological school or an independent theological seminary. In contrast to how you determine the number of students at a particular seminary, you can usually discern whether a seminary is part of a larger university or not by the way ATS displays the name. For the most part, ATS will let you know that this or that school is part of a larger university by including the name of the university after the name of the seminary. If you live in Oklahoma, for example, and you want to attend seminary in state at a university-based school, you only have one option: Oral Roberts School of Theology (www.oru.edu) in Tulsa—the school of theology naturally being an affiliate of the larger university. The other seminary in Oklahoma accredited by ATS, Phillips Theological Seminary (www.ptstulsa.edu), also in Tulsa, is an independent seminary.

Although most university-based seminaries on the ATS website are displayed as such, there are a few exceptions. In Kentucky, for instance, Southern Baptist Theological Seminary (www.sbts.edu), in Louisville, and Asbury Theological Seminary (www.asburyseminary.edu), in Wilmore, are both affiliated with colleges. However, they are not advertised as such. If you would like to attend a seminary that is affiliated with a particular college,

*You can usually
determine whether a
particular seminary
is part of a larger
university by the way
the name is displayed
on the ATS website;
seminaries connected
to colleges may
not be displayed.*

visit the school's website or contact the school directly to find out this information.

III. TYPE OF PROGRAM AND DEGREE

The next two factors that we will discuss are related to the type of program and degree that you will enroll in while at seminary. As discussed in the later chapters on programs and degrees, there are two major types of programs that you can earn: basic or first-professional, and advanced or graduate. (The names of these two types of programs do not appear on your diploma.) If this is your first time at seminary, however, you can enroll only in a basic program. Conversely, you will probably enroll in an advanced program if you have already earned a seminary degree.

Aside from the two types of programs offered at seminaries, there are several types of degrees—each one, of course, falling under the category of basic or advanced program. Because the type of degree you will enroll in is extremely important, you will need to find a school that offers this degree—especially if you are pursuing a more specialized degree such as a doctorate or a degree in counseling. If you are pursuing the most popular of the basic degrees, however (the master of divinity), you will have no problem: almost every seminary offers this degree (and all have the equivalent).

It is fairly easy to determine whether a particular seminary offers the degree that you are interested in. Instead of viewing the different schools according to denomination or geography, for instance, click on the tab labeled "Approved Degrees Offered by Member Schools." This tab will then direct you to a page that contains information about the types of programs and degrees that ATS approves. The programs and degrees are generally classified as follows:

Sample of Programs and Degrees Approved by ATS

Basic Degree Programs		Advanced Degree Programs	
Ministerial	**General Theological (More Academic)**	**Ministerial**	**Teaching/ Research (More Academic)**
Master of divinity	Master of theological studies	Doctor of ministry	Master of (sacred) theology
Master of arts in . . .	Master of arts in . . .	Doctor of missiology	Doctor of theology
Master of (church) music	Master of arts (religion)	Doctor of education	Doctor of philosophy

Although this can get quite confusing if you are new to seminary, briefly read through the different sections at the ATS website, or look at the chart above until you come across the degree that is most appropriate for you. If you have never attended seminary before, it will have to be a degree on the left side of the chart; if you have graduated from seminary before, you will most likely enroll in a degree program on the right side. If you do not find a degree that relates to your professional objectives, spend more time at the ATS website.

After you find a program (basic or advanced) and a specific degree within one of those programs, simply click the type of program you are interested in. This link will direct you to all the seminaries accredited by ATS that offer this degree. Let us say, for instance, that you want to be a counselor or therapist. If you have not already earned a seminary degree, you will be required to enroll in a basic program first. Under the basic programs that are oriented more toward ministerial training, click the link labeled "Specialized Professional Areas." Once you click this, you will connect to a page that contains several degrees for more specialized areas. Scroll down until you find a degree related to counseling or therapy that seems most appropriate for your professional goals (whether a master of arts in [Christian] counseling, a master of arts in marriage and family therapy, or something else). After you come across the appropriate degree, explore the websites of the various seminaries that offer it.

There are two major types of programs offered at seminary: basic or first-professional, and advanced or graduate. You can enroll in an advanced degree only if you have already earned a basic degree.

IV. EDUCATIONAL MODEL (DISTANCE LEARNING)

In contrast to the educational model of seminaries in previous generations, the increasing advance of technology has made many learning formats available. One of the most popular nontraditional educational formats today is distance learning, or distance education. Put simply, distance learning takes place when the student is in a separate location from the instructor or class. If you want to attend seminary but are unable to relocate (and there are no schools in your area that you are interested in), your best option is to earn your degree via distance education. Somewhat confusingly perhaps, distance education does not mean that you can earn your degree *completely* at home—at least not at a seminary accredited by ATS. Instead, distance education means that you can complete a good portion of your degree at home; the other portion must be completed on campus—though your residential requirements are usually for very short periods of time

Distance education means that you can complete a good portion of your degree at home, but you are still required to take occasional courses on campus.

(one to two weeks), and normally not more than a couple of times a year.

If you do decide to enroll in a seminary program via distance education, you will want to click the tab labeled "ATS Institutions Offering Distance Education Courses," which is on the "Member Schools" page that we have been using to explore all the different schools accredited by ATS. Once you are directed to this page, you will see all of the seminaries that provide distance education of some kind or another. Because each school has different programs and requirements, you must investigate the schools on an individual basis.

Just two excellent examples of seminaries that offer programs via distance education are North Park Theological Seminary (www.northpark.edu/sem) in Chicago and Western Theological Seminary (www.westernsem.edu) in Michigan. Explore the websites of some of the other schools for more specific information. But keep in mind that not every school on this page actually offers an entire program via distance education; some may offer only occasional courses.

Other Factors When Deciding on a Seminary

History/Mission	The history or mission of the school is or is not crucial for me.
Housing	I want to live on campus (or off campus).
Finances	The tuition of this school is within my budget.
Faculty	The faculty is (or is not) a major factor for me.
Miscellaneous	I have another factor that I must consider.

Entering Seminary Websites

In contrast to the first list of considerations in the box we discussed earlier, there are some other factors that you may want to think about when looking into different schools, ones that can be considered only by entering the website of a particular school. You cannot determine, for instance, the mission of the school or the tuition costs of the school you are interested in except by navigating its website. For this reason, it will not be possible to take the time to walk through each of the different considerations as we did above; there are simply too many variables and too many seminaries. Instead, I will choose the websites of just two specific schools to give you an example; I encourage you to navigate later the websites of some of the schools that match your individual preferences. The two schools I have chosen are intentionally different in several ways: theologically, geographically, and so forth.

Candler School of Theology of Emory University: Example 1

The first seminary website that we will look through is that operated by Candler School of Theology (www.candler.emory.edu) in Atlanta, which is part of Emory University. Candler is a well-respected school in the mainline tradition (officially part of the United Methodist Church). Of the five factors I have included in the box above, we will begin with the first: history or mission. This can easily be learned. Simply click the tab labeled "About Candler"; once there, you will have several links to connect to for more information about Candler's history and mission. As would be expected, Candler's mission relates in some way to its connection with Emory University. The next two factors, housing and finances, are also readily accessible on the site. Both are found by clicking on the tab labeled "Admissions." There you can find information about both on- and off-campus housing, as well as specific information related to the cost of Candler, and even ways to finance your education.

If you need to earn your degree via distance education, you will have to investigate all the seminaries to locate a school that offers an entire program rather than an occasional class.

The next factor we will consider relates to the faculty members. The faculty members at any given school are very important—perhaps even the most important aspect of the school. If you would like to read about some of the faculty members at Candler to get a feel for their interests and backgrounds, click on the tab labeled "Academics." From there choose the link that takes you to the faculty.

Finally, the last major factor you might want to take into consideration when trying to find the right seminary has to do with your own personal circumstances. Every student comes to seminary with his or her own specific situations; be sure that you know what your circumstances are, and how they will determine where and when you go to seminary.

Gordon-Conwell Theological Seminary: Example 2

The second example of a school that we will look at is Gordon-Conwell Theological Seminary (www.gts.edu), which is located in a small town north of Boston (with affiliate campuses elsewhere). Gordon-Conwell is an interdenominational school of the Protestant evangelical tradition. As we did

ith Candler, we will walk through some of the factors in the box
y be important to you. For information about the mission or history of the school, click the tab labeled "About GCTS." For information on
housing, finances, and faculty, simply click the tab labeled "Campuses," and
then choose which campus you want to attend; you will come across a page
that will prompt you to choose the specific information that you wanted to
learn. Navigate the site further and see what other resources the school may
provide. Both Candler and Gordon-Conwell maintain excellent websites,
so be sure to browse through them for information about these schools in
particular or seminary in general.

Navigating Your Seminary Websites of Choice

As you have probably learned, there are many different factors that
you will need to consider when trying to find the right seminary. We have
just considered many of those factors, and we have looked at two specific
seminaries' websites. Now that you know what to look for, take the time
to navigate some seminary websites that interest you. You can do this by
using the website maintained by ATS.

Ways to Locate Seminary Websites

1. Enter the website maintained by the Association of Theological
   Schools (www.ats.edu).
2. After deciding which factors are most important to you when looking
   for a seminary, search for seminaries by alphabetical order, denomination, geography, types of degrees offered, or by distance learning.
3. Click all those schools that meet your criteria, and then bookmark
   the websites of those schools that seem like the best fit for your circumstances and objectives.

Other Ways to Learn about Specific Seminaries

Because we live in a technological world, we have dedicated most of our
attention to locating seminaries through their respective websites. This
is, after all, the easiest, most direct, most accessible, and cheapest way to
isolate information about any seminary that you would want to know more
about. If for some reason, however, you are unable or simply do not want
to learn about seminaries online, there are more traditional ways of getting to know a particular seminary. In fact, some of these more traditional
ways are actually more informative than navigating the website of a certain

school—particularly if this comes in the form of visiting the school in person or actually speaking with someone who attends the school or who has graduated from it.

The best way to really get to know a seminary is by browsing its seminary website or a brochure and by speaking with someone who attends the school or has graduated from it.

For the most part, there are two ways to learn about a seminary aside from looking at its website. The first is through brochures or catalogs—which are often simply hard copies of the information that you will find on a school's website; the second way to learn about a seminary is by speaking with a person who either attends or works at the school or who graduated from the school—whether by phone, e-mail, or visiting. This second way of getting to know a school is perhaps better. Better yet, a combination of the two ways is the best way of learning about a particular school.

Application Process

The last step that we will discuss in this chapter has to do with the application process. After you have determined which factors are most important to you when deciding on what kind of seminary to attend, and after you have isolated specific schools of interest, you will then need to apply to these schools. Generally speaking, I would recommend applying to at least three seminaries, but probably no more than five or six. (However, all things depend on your individual circumstances.) Often, the application can be completed online, though some schools may have other requirements. The process of applying to a school, however, is more than simply filling out a form. It is essential to take your time and complete all of the requirements as well as possible.

Obtaining and Beginning the Application

It is impossible to say with certainty what the application process will be like for you; there are many variables, ranging from the school you attend to the type of degree you enroll in. Despite these differences, however, there are certain standards and procedures that every school has for admitting and granting scholarships and awards to prospective students. When beginning the application process, start either by logging on to the school's website (look for the words "admissions" or "prospective students") or by contacting the school by e-mail or telephone, to request an application.

However, as you might assume, most schools these days actually provide all the information you need to complete an application via their websites.

Once you download the correct application (there may be several, depending on the program you want to apply to), simply follow the directions. The application process at some schools can be quite lengthy and detailed, because there are many components to the application, and you will need to contact other people and schools for certain items. So you may want to spread out your time across several days (or weeks).

Getting Personal with the Application

You can usually obtain or download an application to a school by browsing the seminary's website. If you do not find an application there or if you prefer to complete it on paper, request one from the school via telephone or e-mail.

As you begin completing your school applications, you will notice very quickly that you are required to provide a good deal of personal information. The reason for this is simple: The application is all that a particular school has when the time comes to admit a prospective student. Although certain schools require visits—and all encourage them—most schools will have to base their acceptance and scholarship decisions entirely on the items that accompany your application. Because this is the case, you will need to be both direct and detailed. Schools will inquire about your college studies, employment history, faith and family background, financial status, ministry experience, and references.

Completing the Application

Because the application process is so detailed, it will probably take you several days or longer to complete it. In addition to the basic information about yourself that you will be able to provide in a short amount of time, there will be at least three other components to the application that will take some time: requesting your official college transcripts to be sent to the seminary, obtaining pastoral and academic references, and writing an essay or two as a writing and academic exercise. Once you have completed the entire application, you will need to sign it, deposit a check for the application fee (you might as well get used to giving the school your money!), and send it off to the school for consideration.

Steps to Follow When Applying to a Seminary

1. Choose those schools (at least a couple) that seem best for your circumstances.
2. Obtain the application (usually online), and apply to each school individually.

3. Complete the application on time, and procure all items required.
4. Have someone proofread your essays and other application materials.
5. Pray with your family and church that God will lead you to the right school.
6. Find out when the school makes admissions decisions, and wait by the mailbox!

Interview or Visitation

Due to the high number of applications that any given school receives, and due to the time limitations of the faculty and staff, many seminaries do not require prospective students to undergo personal interviews or visits to the school in order to be admitted. The more selective schools, however, may have such a requirement. And all schools certainly *encourage* students to visit the campus if they are able. If you do visit the school or have an interview, you will want to be ready with all the questions you may have, and you will want to see whether the school reflects your own interests and preferences.

> *The application is very important when applying to a school, because it is often all that a school has to go on when making admission decisions.*

Things to Think about when Visiting a Seminary

- Visit as many departments as possible (admissions, financial aid, housing).
- Be prepared to ask specific questions.
- Pay special attention to the way people treat you.
- Sit in on a class, and chat with one of the professors or students.
- Walk around the campus and check out the general culture of the school.
- Explore the general area around the school to see whether or not it is comfortable.

Getting Ready for Seminary

It's been exciting writing this chapter, because it is the culmination of the first and second parts of this book, in which we have learned about seminary as well as considered those factors that are most important to you when finding the right school. Although it is very likely that you have still not discovered which school you will attend, I hope that you have made great progress in that direction. However, we still have several other things to consider. In the next section, for instance, we will begin exploring the things you will need to think about while you are in seminary, namely, how to manage your time effectively, what courses you will take, and the differences between the various programs offered.

THINGS TO CONSIDER DURING SEMINARY

9

Managing Your Time, Maintaining Your Faith, and Adjusting to Your New Life

I hope that our discussion in the previous chapters, where we examined many things that you will need to think about before you enter seminary, has been helpful. This chapter begins a new section in the book, where we consider several things during seminary (though each is important to consider before seminary as well). We consider, for instance, how much time you should devote to your studies each semester, issues related to managing time spent with friends and family, and how to maintain your faith while in seminary. We also talk about adjusting to your new life once the semester begins. The reason these things are important is because you can and probably will be distracted at times from family, friends, work—and even your faith—with the pressures and time constraints of seminary. To keep this from happening to you—or at least to minimize how often it occurs—we will discuss each of these issues separately. Finally, the issues we discuss in this chapter are at the center of a seminary education: they will help you decide, if you are still contemplating seminary, whether or not it is right for you.

> *While at seminary you can easily be distracted from family, friends, work, and even your faith with the pressures and time constraints of doing well.*

Managing Your Time

It can seem like everything in life comes down to either time or money. Seminary is no different. If you have neither the time nor the interest to prepare for class each week, think twice before attending seminary! Seminary will take a great deal of your time—much more than you might expect. There will be late nights, for example, as you finish a paper on the rise of monasticism, and there will be times when you have to go to a classmate's house during the weekend to complete a group project. There will be final exams that require an entire week of cramming. And there will be times when you have to decide whether to spend an evening with your family or an evening alone as you— ironically—read a book about Christian community.

Expect to dedicate several hours a week to each class while in seminary—reading roughly 100 pages a week per class.

How much time is required each week for classes and reading? That depends on the person and the program. I have attended some schools that required fifty to sixty hours a week in class and at home preparing for class. I have attended other schools that required considerably less. The time you spend studying also depends on the professor and the class. Every school and every professor will conceive of this differently. You will simply have to allot enough time each week to reasonably manage time spent with family in conjunction with your career as a student. How these come together is something that you and your family must work out. It would be wise to begin thinking about time for school before you start seminary. But after a few weeks of class— when you and your family get accustomed to things—you will have a better understanding of how much time will be required for studying.

Managing Family and School

Time is valuable to everyone, but for those who are married and have children, time can be especially pressing. You do not want your years of seminary to be a blur by the time you graduate. You need to live your life! I have seen extremes in seminary. I am sad to say that I have known seminarians who neglected their spouses and children in order to perform well. In fact, I recently heard from one of my old professors the story of a famous theologian who used to line his office floor with Cheerios so that his child would be occupied while he studied diligently as a graduate student! But I have also known other students who sacrificed a degree of their grades to be more involved with their families. One professor of mine actually worked out a specific schedule while he was in seminary. After each day of class, he went to the library and completed all of his coursework as quickly as possible. Afterward, he went home and spent the evening with his wife and children. He did this so that he would never have to do schoolwork at home. This worked well for him, but it may not work well for you. I could not do what my professor did; I always work from my home, never the library. What is important is that you be aware of these issues now and try to resolve them before they become bigger issues while in seminary.

A piece of professorial advice that I have heard is for married couples to always go to bed together at a regular bedtime. If you do not finish all of your homework the night before, wake up early enough in the morning to complete it then. I think that your marriage will be better if you always try to go to bed when your spouse does. It was certainly not always possible for me to follow this advice, but it was a fine goal to strive for. Figure out what works best for your situation, and make a routine out of it.

If you are married or have children, work out your own schedule with them so that you do not disappear for half a decade of their lives!

Tips on Time and School

- Schedule time for family and friends.
- Think of your time studying as your profession.
- Work hard, but take regular breaks.
- Limit church involvement while in seminary.
- Organize your studies and activities.

How Much Time Is Too Much Time for Studying?

Unfortunately, there is no absolute that you can use to measure whether you are spending too much time or too little time studying. Obviously, neglecting your family and other responsibilities would constitute too much time studying. Conversely, if you flunk out of school because you never completed an assignment, it is a good indication that you did not spend enough time on school!

You should perform your best while in seminary. You are learning a profession, so be sure to learn well. How keen would you be, for instance, if your heart surgeon barely graduated from medical school? You will never have another time like this in your life to devote to learning and study, so use it effectively. Take pride in your vocation and study diligently, but remember your family and other responsibilities too.

66 God will not ask how learned you were in the arts, in languages and in great knowledge, but how you practiced love. 99

Johann Arndt (Lutheran theologian and author)

What about Working during Seminary?

Historically, seminarians often went to school full time and worked only during the summer or throughout the

Questions about Work during Seminary

- Do I need to work while at seminary? If so, will it be part time or full time?
- If I work part time, how many hours a week do I need to work?
- How will my part-time job affect my family time as well as my studies?
- If I work full time, do I want to work in the secular workplace (which probably pays better) or in the Christian workplace (which gives you more experience and is often more flexible)?
- If I work full time, how will I find the time to attend classes, study, and spend quality time with my family and friends?
- How can I prepare right now for balancing my commitments while working and attending seminary? How can I make a schedule that balances all these things?

year as a ministerial intern of some kind. Although some seminarians today do not work at all during the semester, it seems to be more common for students to work at least on a part-time basis concurrently with their studies. In fact, there are many programs these days that actually encourage students to work full time while attending school full time or possibly part time. For those students who do work—whether a few hours a week or fifty—there will be certain pressures that you will most likely face when going to school. One of these will be the question, How much time should I spend at work? As I noted above, it is impossible to answer that question in any systematic way. But there are certain considerations to keep in mind to assist you as you think about this. Read through some of these considerations below, and begin thinking now of how you will juggle your work commitments with other responsibilities.

Maintaining Your Faith

There is another very important yet neglected component to your seminary education. This component may sound peculiar to you at the moment, but I believe that it will become very real to you a semester or two into your studies. What I am referring to is your faith while in seminary. Some students undergo extreme doubt, testing, and general feelings of inadequacy when they attend seminary. Some students also learn and experience so many new things about religion that they begin to question whether their faith is genuine or whether they are truly Christians. Still other students experience no drastic issues of doubt when in seminary, but they do occasionally feel drained spiritually from their classwork and other activities. For these reasons, we will look at ways that you can maintain a healthy spiritual life while in seminary.

Seminary and Growing Pains

Although many people undergo some sort of testing while in seminary, I by no means want to imply that you will lose your faith there. I hope and pray that your seminary experiences will result only in the increasing and maturation of your faith. But, as you may remember from childhood, discomfort is often accompanied by a certain degree of growth. There is a stage of development in human adolescence which people refer to as "growing pains." These are pains that accompany our human development, but they are good and natural in the sense that they are part of the process of human growth.

Seminary can be exhausting not only financially and mentally, but also spiritually.

How to Get Faith-Distracted at Seminary

- You study too much.
- You focus only on academic subjects.
- You question your convictions.
- You are too busy for church.
- You abandon prayer and fellowship.

I would like to suggest that you will probably experience "growth pains of faith" while in seminary. This is, I think, generally a good thing, because you are attending seminary to grow spiritually and learn more about your faith. The potential problem comes when we grow faster than we want to grow. You will sometimes learn something that will cause you to question your faith. Depending on the seminary that you attend, for instance, what you may have been taught in Sunday school could be dismissed as fanciful or naive—a judgment that will sound even more convincing on the lips of the dean of the school or one of your theology professors. Some seminaries, in fact, begin a process of theological deconstruction on first-year students. They identify and eliminate simplistic or simply incorrect notions that students often bring with them to seminary. During the next couple of years of instruction, these schools then help students construct a more historic, coherent, and stable theology.

This can be seen in the way that I have taught classes on biblical interpretation, in which I attempt to deconstruct some of the faulty presuppositions that students have about the Bible. As North Americans, for instance, we tend to approach scripture in a very specific way that differs from how the writers of the Bible and other generations of Christians have approached it. A little deconstruction, when done this way, is a good thing, and it is a vital part of the learning process; however, too much can be devastating to students, and it can cause them to question their faith.

Some seminaries have a twofold process for teaching students: (1) deconstructing faulty assumptions; and then (2) constructing more consistent theological systems.

I am sad to say that some individuals have actually abandoned their faith altogether while in seminary for one reason or another. One of my professors once recounted how a friend abandoned his Christian convictions after years of intense study on the origins of the early church. His friend was simply unable to reconcile what he was learning through history, archaeology, and religion with the faith that he had learned while growing up. As a result, he left the church and has never returned.

Keeping the Faith Alive

However, just because other students have occasionally wandered from the faith as a result of seminary and other rigorous theological study does not mean that you are in danger of abandoning the church once in seminary. It does not even mean that you will encounter minor obstacles along the way. But I do feel confident saying that you will probably experience some discomfort or at least a little uncertainty while at seminary. This need not be a bad thing, however. As I mentioned above, this is part of the learning process. Below are some practical ways that you can maintain a vibrant spiritual life while in seminary.

Keeping Your Spiritual Life Alive while in Seminary

- Pray regularly.
- Meet with classmates on a regular basis, and talk about spiritual issues.
- Schedule time to read the Bible—without any agendas.
- Attend chapel and worship services offered at the seminary.
- Work in a church or other practical ministerial context.
- Speak with professors about spiritual issues they experienced at seminary.
- Take vacations from school and from studying when possible.

Why Your Faith Will Be Tested

One of the greatest theologians in the history of the church, Martin Luther, spoke very openly about spiritual testing. Contrary to what many preach today on television and from pulpits throughout North America, for instance, Luther believed that people went through more spiritual trials and tribulations once they became Christians and once they were engaged in spiritual activities. Luther many times conceived of this struggle as with the devil himself. One of the words he occasionally used to describe some of his personal struggles was the German term *Anfechtung*, which refers to religious despair and restlessness. As a monk Luther had experienced deep despair as he contemplated his relationship to a holy God, and he believed that Christians could never escape temptation and testing while on earth.

New and Difficult Ideas and Concepts

Even though we may not experience the same amount of turmoil that Martin Luther experienced at the internal and spiritual level, most seminarians that I have known have encountered spiritual drainage, uncertainty, and emptiness at one time or another in the midst of their studies. There are many reasons for this. One main reason relates—ironically perhaps—directly to your studies. While in seminary, you will read dozens of books and articles that will cause you to think about issues of faith that you have either never thought of before or that you intentionally avoided because those issues were too difficult or threatening to consider. Your professors will not necessarily pity you; it is their mission to make you think and wrestle with difficult subjects. And it's why you are in seminary.

> 66 Not to lead us to temptation means that God gives us the strength and power to resist. But it does not mean that the spiritual distress is removed and done away with. No one can avoid temptation and enticement as long as we live in the flesh and have the Devil around us, and this will not change: we must bear tribulation, yes, even be in the midst of it. 99
>
> *Martin Luther*

Personal Study

Have you ever had a moment in your life when you knew that the way you had previously understood something was suddenly changing? I have had that experience many times before, and I remember it happening to me once when I was in seminary. I had been reading several books on Christian doctrines, and, in the middle of a particular book, I realized that I had been wrong my entire life about a very important and heavily debated theological concept! I have had many moments like that since then, all of which occurred in the context of personal study.

While in seminary, I believe, you will experience something similar. The way you read the Bible now, for instance, will most likely not be the way you read the Bible after you graduate from seminary. You will see things in a very different light, and this new light will considerably change how you understand God and the world. This should be understood only in a good way, but it will not be long before you are confronted with the reality that what you believed about this or that was simply wrong. You had been wrong; your Sunday school teacher had been wrong; your pastor had been wrong! This may cause you to ponder what else you may be wrong about, and this cycle could go on indefinitely. If I have heard this expression once, I have heard it a dozen times: "I came to seminary with twenty questions and I left with two hundred!"

One reason that seminary may cause a crisis of beliefs is that you are confronted with difficult subjects that you have either intentionally avoided or never even thought about.

The point of seminary is not to learn the answer to every theological question; it is to prepare you for ministry and to equip you with the resources needed to heal this broken world, and to love God and God's creation. Some of your views will change in seminary, but do not allow these changes to lead you to question the basis or authenticity of your faith.

Busyness and Classwork

In the section above we discussed how limited your time will be when you attend seminary. As North Americans, we are busy enough as it is without the added time constraints of studying and working. You will have to devote serious attention to your spiritual life while in seminary. But do not think that you can simply substitute this for a class that you are taking! It doesn't work that way. Your temptation while in seminary will be to neglect your spiritual life, because you are too busy or because you will (wrongly) think that your coursework can take its place. This is misguided; seminary courses may supplement your spiritual diet, but they cannot replace it.

❝ I frequently tell my students that quite a high proportion of what I say is probably wrong, or at least flawed or skewed in some way which I do not at the moment realize. The only problem is that I do not know which bits are wrong; if I did, I might do something about it. ❞

N. T. Wright (Biblical scholar and Anglican bishop)

Academic Focus

I remember having a strange conversation with one of my friends a while after we had graduated from seminary. We were talking about reading the Bible. We both remarked that the Bible came alive to us . . . around a year after we had graduated from seminary! In seminary we had been so preoccupied with concentrating on historical issues, figuring out the meaning in the original languages, finding connections to other biblical letters, and so on that we had missed the bigger picture of God speaking through scripture.

In the third chapter of this book I characterized professional education as being composed of both theoretical and practical components. Although you will certainly be exposed to practical courses and experiences while at seminary, you will probably get the feeling at some point in your studies that your classes are way too academic. This is what happened to my friend and me: we had focused so much on the academic component to reading the Bible that we had little room for the spiritual element. This will probably happen to you as well at some point in your studies if you are not careful and protective of your spiritual life. Below are some suggestions on how to protect yourself.

How to Protect Yourself from Putting Academics above Practical Matters

- Supplement your academic subjects with practical subjects as often as possible.
- Always try to isolate how a seemingly very academic topic—such as election or sin, for instance—relates to faith in a practical way.
- Pray regularly, stay connected to your church, attend worship services at your seminary, and talk with your classmates about how they deal with this issue.
- Take regular breaks when studying to clear your head.

Teachers and Students Who Differ from You

Seminary is a wonderful place, and you will, hopefully, make lifelong friends over the years of your coursework. At the same time, however, you will no doubt come across some eccentric professors and students along the way. Some Christians—even very intelligent and spiritual ones—can be strange birds. While at seminary you will meet students and teachers who will challenge your faith for the very reason that they live so differently from the way that you thought Christians should live. They may say, do, and encourage things that you think are . . . well, unthinkable . . . or at least unusual. During my days at seminary I have come across both teachers and students who have challenged my faith. Some have done so for the better, some for the worse. While you are in seminary, gravitate toward those who challenge you for the better and who will encourage you as you encounter low points in your walk with God. But be prepared to meet and interact with other Christians who will think differently from you— perhaps even extremely so if you attend a seminary beyond your own tradition—and see how you might actually learn from them.

Your temptation while in seminary will be to neglect your spiritual life, because you are too busy or you will (wrongly) think that your coursework can take its place.

Adjusting to Your New Life at Seminary

I remember my first day at the seminary I had just transferred to for my second year. I was in a completely new area geographically; I did not know anyone apart from my wife's family; and I was trying to find a good part-time job. Instead of returning home that first day excited about what I had learned and the new friends that I had made, I felt discouraged. *Did I choose the right seminary? Was I certain I was in the right program?* As the weeks went on and I became immersed in my studies, I realized that I had made the right decision to attend that seminary and enroll in that program. Eventually I made friends, found a job, secured a nice house to live in, and even found the area preferable to where I had been living—who knew that East Texas was not Utopia after all? However, this transition did not occur overnight; it took weeks—possibly even months—before I adjusted to seminary and this new phase of my life.

For some of you, this adjustment may prove difficult. This is especially true if you have a spouse and children, are moving to a new area, have been out of school for many years, or find change hard. For others, the transition to seminary will be much more fluid, even exhilarating. Whereas the first two sections in this chapter focused on adjusting to school with reference to time and your faith, this section will consider other more external issues related to adjusting to seminary—particularly for those who will need to relocate.

Exploring the New Area

One of the first things that you will want to do once you have decided on a seminary is to explore the area around it. You will want to get to know the general vicinity of that neighborhood or area of town. Are there convenient stores? Is this neighborhood safe? Is there parking or is public transportation easily accessible? How far is the school from my house? These are questions that you will need to ask even if you are not relocating. If you are relocating, you will naturally need to think about a host of other questions: What is this town like? Are there any parks, museums, or malls in the area? Where is a post office? Where should I shop for groceries and clothes? And—for you Southerners—where is the nearest Mexican restaurant?

Finding a Church

If you find yourself in a new area in order to attend seminary, one of your priorities will be to find the right church to get involved with. What type of church you decide to attend depends on a number of factors. If, for example, you are part of a specific denomination—and especially if you intend to be ordained within it—you will probably want to locate a church in that denomination. Even if you do not intend to be ordained or become a pastor, however, it is still recommended that you find a church most closely associated with your own tradition: whether Catholic, Orthodox, or Protestant. If you are in a small town or simply unable to attend a church related to your tradition, make whatever decision you think is best—unless of course that decision is to not attend any church while in seminary (you would be surprised at how often this occurs). You may also want to make this decision based on additional factors: How far is this church from my house or the seminary? Is the church too big or too small? Do I get along with the worship style, the pastor, and the rest of the congregation?

> **Questions for New Area**
> - Is there adequate parking?
> - Is this neighborhood safe?
> - How far is the school from my house?
> - Where is the nearest Mexican restaurant?

One other thing that you may want to consider when looking for a church is a job or internship opportunity related to that church. Depending on what your professional objectives are upon graduating from seminary, you will need some experience while you are in school. Churches are wonderful places for seminarians to acquire experience. This experience may come in the form of a part- or full-time job, an internship, or simply the opportunity to teach Sunday school, be involved in worship, lead a missions trip, or organize pot-luck dinners. Just be sure that you are comfortable with the church, and that it will enable you to get involved and get some experience while in school.

Meeting People

Perhaps the most important component to a great seminary experience is the people that you meet along the way. I have been blessed during the years that I have been involved with seminary by the many people that I have come across—whether staff, faculty, or students. While you are in seminary, I would encourage you to take the time to get to know your professors and your classmates. This makes sense not only because you will all have so much in common and because you will spend most of your time with these people for the next several months of your life, but also because your friendships in seminary will hopefully last much longer than the length of your studies. I am still good friends, for instance, with

Finding a church is one of the first things that you will need to do if relocating for seminary.

a number of students and professors that I met while in seminary. In fact, spending time with them and their families outside of class has been one of the most rewarding aspects of my seminary experience. While in school, take the time to get to know those around you by inviting people over for dinner, by getting involved in any extracurricular activities offered at the school, or simply by making yourself accessible to others. The friendships you will make will be worth the effort.

Family Matters

One more thing that you may need to consider if you are relocating for seminary has to do with your family. If you are married and have children, your spouse and your children will probably have a more difficult time adjusting than you will. After all, you will be the one meeting new people, having new experiences, taking exciting classes, and preparing for your career through work or internships. During this time your family may feel lonely and out of place. If so, you will have to implement some of the strategies that I mentioned above with regard to balancing time and family. This transition may take a while, but keep at it.

Summarizing

If I had to summarize this chapter in one word, I would choose the word *proactive*. This chapter is about being proactive when it comes to seminary and organizing your life while you are a student. If you don't do so yourself, I guarantee you that someone or something else will! There are three main ways that I referred to this organization: time, faith, and adjustment.

While in school, take the time to get to know those around you by inviting people over for dinner, by getting involved in any extracurricular activities offered at the school, or simply by making yourself accessible to others.

You will first need to be proactive about your time, for everything will be vying for it: classes, homework, family, friends, work, and pets. You will have to schedule and plan in advance. You will have to plan, for instance, how many hours you will work a week; how many hours you will spend studying; how much time you will spend with your family and friends; and how many hours you will spend text-messaging!

You will also have to be proactive concerning your faith and your spiritual life. Although you should certainly become a deeper and more faithful Christian while at school, your seminary is not ultimately responsible for your relationship with God. Nor is it necessarily responsible for all of your theological beliefs. These aspects of your life are related to but ultimately separate from seminary. For this reason, you will need to intentionally protect your spiritual health while in seminary.

Finally, there is the issue of adjustment. Seminary will perhaps take a good deal of adjusting to get used to. If you are married or have children, your family will need to adjust too. You will possibly have to adjust to being in a new area, learning your way around town, finding a new church, and generally orienting yourself to a new way of life. This may take some time. For me, the first month in particular was not as easygoing and enjoyable as I had anticipated. I had to overcome being in a new area, a new program, a new house—a new everything. This was exciting in one sense, but it took some adjustment as well. In the next chapter we will continue our discussion of things to consider during seminary by adjusting to technology and classroom instruction.

10

Technology and Classroom Instruction at Seminary

In the previous chapter we talked about some of the ways you can prepare yourself for seminary by organizing your time effectively and by maintaining a healthy spiritual life. In this chapter, we continue our discussion about being prepared for seminary by learning about what to expect with regard to technology and seminary education. We will also discuss several types of seminary coursework. Although most seminaries are financially unable to maintain the latest available technology, they are becoming increasingly dependent upon technology, integrating the advances of technology into the way they educate their students. This chapter outlines some of the ways that technology has entered the seminary classroom, so that you will know what to expect as you begin your first semester. This chapter will additionally prepare you for the next two chapters, which discuss the type of classes you will take while in seminary.

Seminary Lesson 101: Technology is very important in seminary. Be prepared to work in this technological environment.

Technology

The staff at seminaries today is very different from the staff of seminaries during the nineteenth and twentieth centuries. Obviously, there are still

125

presidents and deans and theology professors, just as there was a century ago. But the staff is much more specialized, and it is made up of many personnel who have no official training in theology. Instead of doctorates in theology, many employees have degrees in business or finance. In fact, one of the most interesting developments in recent years has been the addition of staff that is specialized in computers and technology. Certain seminaries even employ entire departments devoted to the maintenance of technology.

This is just the beginning. In the ensuing years technology will continue to be an extremely important component to education—theological or otherwise. Although it would be an exaggeration to say that future innovations in technology will completely change the way seminaries teach their students, technology certainly will be and already has been a factor in how students learn and are taught at seminaries. Below we will look at just some of the changes that technology has produced in seminary education.

Classroom Instruction

The first change that we will look at has to do with classroom instruction. In one of the colleges where I have taught, each student received his or her own laptop computer during the first semester of school. In the old days teachers began class with, "Please take out paper and pencil"; today's teachers have to ask students to turn off their computers or to log off the Internet during lecture. Computers, like iPods and cellular phones, are ubiquitous—even at seminaries. Many students will bring laptops with them to class and use them to—purportedly—take notes. In fact, most all seminaries encourage computer use by students. Many seminaries today provide wireless Internet connections for their students, and many faculty members have changed their teaching styles along with the changes in computer-based technology. Both teacher and student use computers as much in the classroom today as outside the classroom.

What this means, practically speaking, is that seminary education is much more dispersed and less centralized. In the traditional model of education, the professor transferred information orally to students, who then wrote down the information on paper. Today attention is directed less toward the professor and more toward the students, and perhaps even more toward the medium of technology, whether the computer or a related device. Recently I was in a classroom where the professor made a historical error. One clever student, who happened to be connected to the wireless Internet connection at the school, detected the error and quickly corrected the professor after locating the correct answer! This ability to access information so quickly affects the way we educate and learn. Though it is certain that seminarians will always be studying the Bible and other related Christian documents and materials, what will change is the way we study these things. The following are some of the more common ways that technology has been integrated into seminary classrooms and instruction.

BLACKBOARD

Over the past few years many seminaries have begun using Blackboard, which is a computer learning system (and also the name of the software company) that manages and facilitates classroom learning and instruction. Today few seminaries do not use their program or a related computer software system for class activities or e-learning. Through Blackboard, students are able to communicate directly with each other and have discussions about related class materials and assignments. Instructors use Blackboard in any number of ways: to display students' grades, pose questions, submit assigned readings, make class announcements, and monitor students' interactions. At one of the seminaries that I have attended, all incoming students were required to attend a month-long orientation to technology. One of the first things we learned was how to operate Blackboard. I would expect this type of computer usage to continue in the future.

POWERPOINT

Traditionally, the professor was the center of the learning experience; the students were the recipients of his or her knowledge. Today that is different in many classrooms. Faculty members often use computer-based programs when they teach—one such example being PowerPoint, a computer software program that can be used for compiling information and presenting it in a useful and manageable way. Professors use this program to present information in a way that allows them to teach without necessarily becoming the central focus of the classroom. In fact, many seminary classes are organized in such a way that students make just as many presentations as the teacher.

RADIO, MOVIES, AND TELEVISION

In a class that I once took in seminary on the intersection of film and theology, we watched dozens of movies, both in and out of class. The idea of offering such a class a few decades ago—particularly at the seminary level—would have been unimaginable. Today it is not. Some seminary professors incorporate movies, television, and even radio clips into instruction. This will no doubt be an area that receives further attention in future seminary education. More and more professors will begin incorporating clips from television, movies, and the news, or excerpts from songs, into their teaching—as a way to facilitate learning as well as to better understand the culture in which we live.

Online Courses

The second change in seminary that technology has produced is the increase of online courses. Recently I heard on the radio of a university that started teaching an economics course on the Internet. Actually, the entire class was a computer-generated game that students played online! Throughout the course the students regularly discussed what they were learning via Blackboard, and the professor graded their work at the end of the semester according to how well they played the game. Online courses are becoming increasingly popular at schools these days, even at seminaries. In fact, many courses at seminary that are traditional in the sense that they are offered in a normal classroom setting have additional online require-ments. Other courses are conducted entirely online. Such classes may either cater to a distance-learning format—the student takes the online class hundreds of miles away from the seminary—or be taken by a student living on campus. In this respect, online courses vary from class to class and school to school.

There are no seminaries accredited by ATS that offer degrees exclusively online; a portion of classes must be given on campus.

Although online courses are becoming more popular with each year, I do not foresee that seminary education will one day be conducted completely online. In fact, as far as I know, there are no ATS accredited seminaries that provide degrees *exclusively* online. Certain classes or even major portions of a student's degree may be conducted online, but it is not possible at this time to earn a complete degree online—at least not at a fully ATS-accredited seminary. Online courses, however, are becoming increasingly popular with schools and students, and it is likely that there will be an increase in online courses offered at seminaries in the future.

Distance Education

The third change in seminary education facilitated technology is what is called distance education or distance learning. Distance education takes place when the student is in a different location (off-site rather than on-site) than the professor and the class. There are currently dozens of seminaries in North America that provide distance education in one way or another. Reformed Theological Seminary (www.rts.edu), for instance, in Jackson,

Mississippi, offers distance education through its "virtual campus" that enables certain students to pursue a master's degree in seminary largely (but not entirely) from home—with minimal on-site instruction. There are other such programs across North America, and, as was the case above with regard to online courses, there will probably be even more schools that provide such learning in the ensuing years.

However, as I stated above, there is no seminary accredited by ATS that offers a degree by distance education alone in the sense that you never have to leave your home. Instead, students interested in distance education are required to spend a specific amount of time on campus for the completion of their degree. Generally, about one-half of a master of arts degree and two-thirds of a master of divinity must be conducted on site in order to meet the criterion set forth by ATS (see www.ats.edu for specific information). Such courses are offered in many ways: through DVDs, MP3s, CD-ROMs, cassette tapes, the Internet, and mail. If you are in need of distance education while in seminary, consult your seminary of interest to learn about more specific requirements and offerings.

Regent University School of Divinity (www.regent.edu/acad/schdiv), in Virginia Beach, is an example of an established school that offers innovative and flexible programs for seminarians in need of distance education. They offer various master's and doctoral degrees. There are many other seminaries in North America that offer similar programs. For example, Bethel Seminary of the East (http://seminary.bethel.edu), an affiliate of the main campus in St. Paul, Minnesota, is another seminary that offers very flexible degrees that can be earned without having to relocate.

Certain seminaries maintain one or more extension campuses that are located in a different region and are usually smaller and not as developed. The extension campus may have its own faculty or utilize faculty from the main campus.

In addition to distance education, there are several seminaries in North America that operate extension sites. These are campuses that offer education on site; however, they differ from traditional campuses in that students are sometimes in need of attending the larger campus for a portion of their studies to complete their degree. In other words, students at extension campuses may be able to complete many of their courses in their area, but will often need to attend the parent seminary campus for certain courses. It all depends on the size and resources of the extension campus. Gordon-Conwell Theological Seminary (www.gts.edu), outside of Boston, for instance, is a very large and respected seminary that offers an extension site in Jacksonville, Florida—in cooperation with its other daughter campus in Charlotte, North Carolina.

These extension sites differ from multiple campuses in that seminaries that operate multiple campuses offer entire degrees on site. In this way, Gordon-Conwell Theological Seminary (www.gts.edu) operates three campuses: the main campus in South Hamilton, Massachusetts; an urban campus in Boston; and another campus in Charlotte, North Carolina. These three campuses each offer entire degrees; the extension site in Florida will probably eventually offer all degrees on campus and will thus be another campus in its own right.

Courses Today That Reflect the Culture

Another change in seminary education today, aside from technology, has to do with the types of courses that are offered. Unlike seminary several years ago, many students today take a portion of their classes during the summer, at night, online, by extension, or via intensive classes that last anywhere from a weekend to a month. An increasing number of students are also attending seminary on a part-time basis. The traditional three-year, full-time model of seminary education is not as dominant as it used to be. Even those students who do attend seminary full time often take classes in nontraditional formats. Such formats accord well with the North American mentality of convenience and a culture that esteems expediency.

Many seminarians today take a portion of their classes during the summer, at night, online, by extension, or via intensive classes.

Many seminaries, in fact, have adapted to the prevailing culture and have experienced tremendous success with these nontraditional formats and new types of courses. Biblical Theological Seminary (www.biblical.edu) outside of Philadelphia, for example, has pioneered several flexible and inventive programs that try to engage the culture in which it finds itself. The school offers both a three-year master of divinity degree and a two-year master of arts degree in counseling that allows students to simultaneously work full time and complete their seminary education in a flexible format. In this section we will discuss some of those different formats in relation to seminary courses.

Concentrated and Intensive Courses, and Modular Courses

The first format that we will discuss refers to what are called concentrated or intensive courses. A concentrated or intensive course is one that does not distribute classroom time into the traditional weekly or biweekly schedule across an entire semester of three to four months. Instead, the classes are concentrated in a specific way. How they are intensified or concentrated depends on the nature of the course and school. I have taken a couple of seminary courses, for example, that lasted an entire week—from the morning until the afternoon each day of the week. Other concentrated courses that I have taken were weekend courses, which were offered Friday nights and Saturday mornings and afternoons for a series of three to four weeks. Similar formats for concentrated courses are terms in January and summer sessions (traditionally times set aside for vacation or holidays). These are very popular formats, as they enable students who may otherwise be unable to attend seminary to take classes that comport with their family time, schedules, and jobs.

Some programs are divided into specific cohorts or groups of students who take all of their classes together through the entirety of their seminary degrees.

Courses that are related to intensive classes are modular courses, which are courses that integrate Internet learning with classroom learning. Instead of students working entirely at home or on campus, in other words, instruction is divided into two parts. Frequently, the first part is conducted at home, while the second part is conducted at the campus via an intensive course. Modular courses are very popular at seminaries, largely because they combine flexibility with classroom time.

Specialized Practical Courses

Another recent phenomenon in seminary education has to do with the increase in practical courses. In contrast to the first seminaries in the nineteenth century, which were more academically oriented, many seminaries today provide students with a wide range of course selections related to practical ministry and more pragmatic concerns. Most seminaries offer courses, for instance, in counseling, spiritual disciplines, and spiritual formation, and more specific courses related to pastoral and practical ministry. In fact, the popularity of the doctor of ministry degree—a popular graduate degree for those who already have a master of divinity from seminary—is proof in itself that seminaries are increasingly interested in offering more practical or ministerial courses.

A concentrated or intensive course is one that is conducted on campus for an intensive and abbreviated time period.

Bethel Seminary (http://seminary.bethel.edu) in St. Paul, for example, offers a master of arts in community ministry leadership, and a master of arts in global and contextual studies; Columbia Theological Seminary (www.ctsnet.edu) in Georgia offers a doctor of ministry, doctor of educational ministry, and doctor of theology

A modular course is one that is divided into online or home learning and on-campus learning.

in pastoral care and counseling; Erskine Theological Seminary (www.erskineseminary.org) in South Carolina offers a master of arts in practical ministry.

Cultural and Elective Courses

The last change in seminary education that we will discus is the shift from more required courses to more elective courses—particularly courses related to culture. A few years ago, for instance, I heard about a college that began teaching a course on the intersection between philosophy and the television series *The Simpsons*. Although I have never heard of such a course being offered at seminary, seminaries are moving in a similar direction. More and more courses are being offered each year distinct from the traditional curriculum of biblical studies, theology, and church history. Many seminaries currently offer more culturally embedded courses that, I assume, would have been unheard-of a century ago: the relation of cinema to theology; the writings of C. S. Lewis or J. R. R. Tolkien and the gospel; women in the church; postmodernity and preaching; the relation of science to theology; and so on. Recently, one of the seminaries that I graduated from has offered a course on *The Da Vinci Code* each year, which has been a very successful class.

Trinity Evangelical Divinity School (www.tiu.edu/divinity), outside of Chicago, for another example, offers classes in bioethics, the thought of C. S. Lewis, the theology of Jonathan Edwards, and the history of missions in China. Claremont School of Theology (www.cst.edu), in southern California, offers courses related to ethical questions of war, women in the Book of Genesis, and gender and sexuality.

Putting Together Seminary, Technology, and Classroom Instruction

The seminary of the twenty-first century is certainly different in many ways from previous generations of schools. The main reasons for these changes have to do with the constant advancement of technology and our shifting culture. While you are preparing yourself for seminary, be mindful of the ways that technology and even the culture have changed the way classes are conducted and how they have determined what types of classes you will have to take. In the following two chapters we will continue our discussion about classroom instruction by focusing on the different types of classes that you will take while in seminary.

11

Coursework and Classes

Biblical Studies and Systematic Theology

We have seen that seminary is not necessarily going to be an easy or carefree time in your life. In this respect, seminary is like other professional schools and graduate programs. Where seminary differs from other programs is in relation to the types of classes that you will take. Specifically, we will concern ourselves in this chapter with biblical studies and systematic theology; the next chapter will focus on church history and practical theology.

> 66 A theological school is a place where Scripture and the classics of theological response to Scripture are read in common to the end of the formation of Christian intellectual habits. 99
>
> *John Webster*
> *(theologian and author)*

Required and Elective Courses

As you probably remember from college, each educational degree is comprised of both required courses and a certain number of elective courses. Seminary is no different. Every program usually entails a combination of required and elective courses—with an emphasis on the required ones. An example of a required course would be an introduction to the New Testament. An example of an elective would be a class on the theology of Dietrich Bonhoeffer. Typically, there are fewer elective courses offered at seminary as a result of size—although larger schools and the contemporary trend of seminary education allow for many electives. Regent College (www. regent-college.edu), in Vancouver, for instance, offers a master of divinity that largely contains required courses, while offering several elective courses and concentrations as well. In this section I will give examples of both required and elective courses. I base these courses on the most popular degree, the master of divinity.

Seminaries offer both required and elective courses, though the former are more common.

Fourfold Division of Seminary Courses

For our purposes we will break down seminary coursework into the four principal areas of theology—a convention of theological education that has been in place for many years. These four components of theology proper are: (1) biblical studies, (2) systematic theology, (3) church history, and (4) and practical theology. Every program at seminary contains components of these four subjects—varying from school to school and program to program. Note: some schools may not use this exact terminology. Below we will discuss these four disciplines in depth as well as their related subdisciplines.

Fourfold Division of Seminary Courses

Biblical studies	Old Testament and New Testament; Hebrew and Greek
Systematic theology	Systematic ordering and understanding of the Christian faith
Church history	Study of doctrine, documents, events, and persons in the church's past
Practical theology	Embodying and applying the truths of Christianity to our lives

Biblical Studies

In biblical studies the focus is on the Bible (no surprise there!). These classes concern themselves with either the Old Testament or the New Testament—rarely, what is sometimes called the intertestamental literature, the Jewish books written (you guessed it!) between the Old and New Testaments. Classes in biblical studies introduce you to the historical, social, textual, and theological issues involved in each of the different books in the Bible. However, don't expect a Sunday school lesson on Jonah and the whale while in seminary. Seminaries presuppose that you know the biblical stories. Instead of spending time *in* the text, in other words, you often spend much of your time *around* the text. I remember a conversation a friend and I had one day after enduring a gruesome lecture about the culture of the Akkadians in a class on the Old Testament: "You know," he said to me, "if I had known that we were not going to actually study the Bible in seminary I would have gone to a Bible college instead." Although I understood his frustration, it is important to realize that seminary courses do make a difference when it comes to reading, understanding, and teaching the Bible.

Courses in biblical studies endeavor to teach you the art and science of biblical interpretation (called *hermeneutics*) and to provide you with the tools necessary for future study when the time arises to understand the Bible on your own and teach it to others. But these courses do not necessarily teach you *the Bible*. Rather, they teach you about the cultures of the Akkadians, Babylonians, Greeks, Israelites, and Romans. They teach you about the history of the interpretation of the Bible and how the Bible was formed. They teach you when the books were most likely written, and in what context, and what the authors sought to accomplish by writing them.

> **Biblical Studies**
> -
> - Old and New Testaments
> - How to interpret the Bible
> - Historical background
> - Basics of Hebrew and Greek
> - Content of individual books

OLD TESTAMENT

The Old Testament is the first part of the Christian Bible. In contemporary Christian editions it consists of thirty-nine books. These books describe in great detail the religious history of the nation of Israel. Sometimes referred to as the Hebrew Scriptures, this corpus of texts has been traditionally divided into three subsections by Jews: (1) Torah, (2) Prophets, and (3) Writings. Christians, however, often divide the Old Testament differently: (1) Pentateuch, (2) Historical Books, and (3) Poetic and Prophetic Books. Most seminaries follow some variation of this latter threefold division. What is more, many seminaries offer an introductory course to the Old Testament. Such a course is basic and generally surveys the story and stories of the Old Testament. Attention is usually directed to issues of biblical interpretation, questions of culture and history, and how the Old Testament is meant to be understood in our contemporary context.

The Old Testament is sometimes referred to as the "Hebrew Scriptures" or, rarely, the "First Testament." The Old Testament is an assortment of books written about God's relationship with Israel.

Pentateuch / Torah

The Torah (or Pentateuch, in Greek) refers to the first five books of the Bible: Genesis through Deuteronomy. The word *torah* is a term with essentially two meanings: "instruction" or "law" in Hebrew, and a more general designation of referring to the first five books of the Old Testament. These biblical books—the Torah—have special importance in Jewish and Christian thinking, because they serve as the foundation for the rest of the Bible, particularly the Old Testament. The Torah begins with creation, describes the development and history of the nation of Israel and the giving of the law on Mount Sinai, and concludes with Moses's speech to the Israelites before they cross the Jordan River and enter the Promised Land.

The Torah and the Pentateuch refer to the same five books: Genesis, Exodus, Leviticus, Numbers, and Deuteronomy.

Historical Books

Typically, the books specified as historical are those from Joshua through Esther. A class dedicated to these books will focus on the historical background to each of these texts and how one ought to read biblical narrative. You will look at figures such as Joshua, Deborah, Samuel, and David, as well as Samson and Delilah. You will also discuss Israel's disobedience to God's covenant, the establishment of the monarchy in Israel, the division of the twelve tribes, the exile, and the return from exile.

Poetic and Prophetic Books

The final Old Testament section is sometimes divided into two parts: the poetic and the prophetic. The poetic books—from Job through Song of Songs—are composed almost exclusively of Hebrew poetry, and they generally address issues of wisdom and knowledge. The prophetic books are fifteen in number—from Isaiah through Malachi. These books are also mostly poetic, though several of them have portions of prose narrative. Many seminaries combine both the poetic and prophetic materials into one course because of the similar features they share. The major themes of such a course would be the following: how to read and characterize biblical poetry, understanding how wisdom functions in Israel, discerning the relation of Israel to the covenant, and the nature of prophecy in the ancient Near East.

You might be surprised to learn that poetry makes up almost half of the Old Testament.

NEW TESTAMENT

The New Testament is a collection of twenty-seven documents written in Greek about the life and ministry of Jesus of Nazareth. Practically all of the New Testament authors were of Jewish background and they all presupposed the truth of the Old Testament. Although each of the authors of these books emphasized different things, they all wrote under the conviction that Jesus Christ had changed the course of all history as a result of his teachings and resurrection from the dead. Many seminaries divide these books into three general courses: (1) Gospels, (2) Acts and Paul, and (3) the General Epistles and Revelation. In addition, as was the case with the Old Testament, most seminaries offer an introductory course on the New Testament. These courses typically concentrate on basic issues about Jesus, the Jewish and Greco-Roman background in the first century, the use of the Old Testament by the New Testament, and general questions relating to biblical interpretation.

Gospels

Formally, there are four Gospels: Matthew, Mark, Luke, and John. The Gospels concentrate on the life, teachings, and work of Jesus of Nazareth. They have always played an important role in Christianity, because they alone contain the teachings and ministry of Jesus. In modern categories they are similar to biographies of Jesus—yet with the express purpose of eliciting faith in the reader. The first three of these Gospels share several features and are thus regarded as the Synoptic Gospels. These three are interpreted together and seem to be structured in similar ways. The Synoptic Gospels contrast with the Gospel of John, which portrays Jesus in a different manner. In a course on the Gospels, expect to concentrate on the following: the person of Jesus and his relation to the church, how the Gospels took shape, what the kingdom of God means in each of the books, and how one interprets the Gospels in comparison to each other ("the Synoptic Problem").

The Gospels are the only biblical documents that recount the life of Jesus.

Acts and Pauline Letters

In addition to the Gospels, the book of Acts and the letters of Paul have traditionally been highly regarded in the church. The writer of the book of Luke wrote a companion volume to his Gospel, the book of Acts—a book that begins immediately after Jesus's resurrection from the dead in Jerusalem, and which ultimately ends with the apostle Paul preaching the gospel to the world in Rome. For this reason, it is only logical to combine a course on Acts with the writings of Paul, whose letters immediately follow the book of Acts in the Bible. Thirteen letters are attributed to Paul in the New Testament—the first being the letter to the Romans and the last three (apart from Philemon) being what are frequently referred to in seminary as the Pastoral Epistles: 1 and 2 Timothy, and Titus. Seminary courses that treat Acts and Paul together usually accentuate the following: the change from Jewish to Gentile

Christianity; the role of the Holy Spirit in Acts; the life and missionary journeys of the apostle Paul; as well as chief concerns of Paul's such as justification, new life in Christ, faith and works, and relations between Jews and Gentiles.

General Epistles and Revelation

For good or ill, the last section of books in the New Testament has traditionally been the most neglected. These books are sometimes divided into three categories: (1) the Book of Hebrews, (2) the Catholic or General Epistles, (3) and the Book of Revelation. The letter to the Hebrews is positioned immediately after Paul's letters because it was historically attributed to Paul. However, few today believe that Paul wrote this letter, which emphasizes the relation of Jesus to the Old Testament sacrificial system.

The words epistle *and* letter *are roughly equivalent when speaking about the books of the New Testament that were written to specific communities.*

The Catholic Epistles are seven in number—1 Peter through Jude. Their name derives from the Greek word that means "according to the whole" or "universal" because they were not addressed to specific communities, as Paul's letters were. Rather, they were addressed to a more general and disparate audience of Christian communities across the Mediterranean. These seven epistles are probably the least popular books in the New Testament—having been overshadowed by the Gospels and Paul's letters. In contrast to the neglect of the Catholic Epistles, however, stands the Book of Revelation. Although it is the last book in the New Testament, historically it has been one of the church's favorites. It is considered by many scholars to be the most difficult book in the New Testament to interpret; as a result, it has always been one of the *most* interpreted.

Sample of Seminaries Offering Degrees in Biblical Studies

Seminary	Degree
Capital Bible Seminary (www.bible.edu)	Master of Arts in Biblical Studies
Grand Rapids Theological Seminary (http://grts.cornerstone.edu)	Master of Arts in Old Testament Master of Arts in New Testament
Midwestern Baptist Theological Seminary (www.mbts.edu)	Master of Arts in Biblical Archaeology Master of Arts in Biblical Languages
Western Seminary (www.westernseminary.edu)	Master of Arts in Exegetical Theology

Biblical Languages (Required or Elective)

The third and final component to the discipline of biblical studies is the biblical languages. Contrary to what you may have heard, several scholars believe that neither Moses nor the apostle Paul knew English! To get to the original languages of the Bible, therefore, many seminaries require at least one or two courses in each of the biblical languages—Hebrew and Greek, respectively. (Latin is not a biblical language.) Still other schools are moving away from this model and no longer require their students to take the original languages, because many people are intimidated—if not downright frightened—by the notion of having to study Greek or Hebrew! If the thought of learning Hebrew makes you want to jump off a mountain, perhaps you should find a school that does not require the biblical languages for a degree. Or, if you really want to be bold, go ahead and take Hebrew or Greek anyway. Having taught Greek to seminary students before, I can honestly say that by the time the course is over they are usually delighted that they have taken the time to learn it.

I once had a friend in seminary who left the master of divinity program because she simply could not pass Hebrew. Instead of quitting seminary, however, she entered a master of arts degree that was practical in nature and did not require the languages. Conversely, I had another friend from a different seminary who also could not seem to pass Hebrew. He had two options. One was to transfer his credits to a school that did not require Hebrew (the school we attended required the biblical languages for every program). The second option was to take Hebrew again. He took the latter option, and, as he has stated, he is better off for it.

The Bible was written in three different languages: Hebrew, Aramaic, and Greek. The first two were the written languages for the Old Testament, while Greek was used for the New Testament. Aramaic, however, is not offered in seminary courses—except in advanced or elective courses. The reason is twofold. First, Aramaic represents a very small portion of the Old Testament (it is found, for example, in sections of Daniel and Ezra); second, it is a cognate language to Hebrew, which means that the two are very similar. Classes in the biblical languages of Hebrew and Greek are introductory. They are meant to introduce you to the rudiments of these languages, mostly through learning vocabulary, grammar, and interpretive strategies. If learning the languages is required for your particular program, then you will usually take one or two classes per language. Many schools, however, combine a

Hebrew is written from right to left, which is the opposite of Western languages, like English and Latin.

year's worth of work into only one course per language—which makes for a very long semester indeed!

Systematic Theology

The second division of seminary curriculum after biblical studies is theology proper. Frequently this discipline is labeled "systematic theology," to separate it from the general word *theology*—which can be a vague term as a result of its ability to encompass all of seminary curriculum. Systematic theology attempts to make logical sense out of the Christian theological enterprise. It is the systematic ordering of the Christian faith into distinct categories that can be understood and applied. Depending on what type of school you go to, it is like putting the Bible into an encyclopedia. Take, for instance, the idea of sin. Systematic theology would look through the Bible for any possible reference to sin. Afterward, it would synthesize the findings and try to figure out what the Bible (in addition to other related disciplines) teaches about it.

> 66 Systematic theology . . . [has] the contemporary task of gathering together the elements of our faith into a coherent whole. 99
>
> *Richard Muller (historical theologian and author)*

Systematic theology would include examining the teachings about essentially everything: God, Jesus, the Trinity, justification, forgiveness, sexuality, marriage, and even the Bible itself. Systematic theology offers boundaries and provides coherence to theology. It attempts to articulate the nature of reality according to Christian categories. Systematic theology can be a very abstract discipline. Many schools, however, have incorporated more practical aspects into these courses.

SYSTEMATIC THEOLOGY I AND II (OR EVEN III)

The typical seminary program will require two to three classes in systematic theology. These classes are variously divided and entitled. I have therefore not included a specific title for the course. Some schools utilize old distinctions such as the "doctrine of God," the "doctrine of humanity," or the "doctrine of the Holy Spirit." Others use even more technical titles, such as "soteriology" (the study of salvation) or "ecclesiology" (the study of the church) or "pneumatology" (the study of the Holy Spirit).

Regardless of the terminology, however, these courses will classify the nature of theology into many different categories, which will then be studied according to those classifications. If a class is entitled "Soteriology," for example, it will discuss the nature of salvation, that is, how a person becomes and remains a Christian. It would include terms like *justification* (how a person becomes a Christian) and *sanctification* (how a person remains a Christian). The class would also take into consideration passages from the Bible that deal with these concepts, and it would discuss what other theologians have written on these topics. Studying the development of doctrines may also constitute a portion of these classes.

Other traditional terms for systematic theology are "dogmatic theology" or even "doctrinal theology."

ETHICS (REQUIRED OR ELECTIVE)

The discipline of ethics is often included under the area of theology or systematic theology. However, it also shares many features with practical theology and is therefore subsumed under this discipline at some schools. Either way, a course on ethics focuses on understanding the relation between theology and practice. In other words, it presupposes that there is a dynamic relationship between what one believes and how one lives as a Christian. Ethics is more than morality; it takes into consideration the whole person and how a life lived in obedience to Jesus involves complex decisions and relationships. Ethics is an important field in seminary. Certain schools take this discipline very seriously and require it for all seminarians while others incorporate its contents into other courses such as systematic or practical theology.

66 The knowledge of good and evil seems to be the aim of all ethical reflection. The first task of Christian ethics is to invalidate this knowledge. 99

Dietrich Bonhoeffer (German theologian and martyr)

PHILOSOPHY (REQUIRED OR ELECTIVE)

Many seminaries and divinity schools offer classes in philosophy. The relation between philosophy and theology has always been a very close one. Throughout the medieval church theology was construed as the "queen of the sciences" with philosophy serving as her "maidservant." Philosophy also served as an important component to seminary education at the inception of seminaries in the sixteenth century. Although this approach is still followed by many today, others have been abandoned it altogether. Whatever the case, philosophy does play a role in theology and your seminary of choice will probably offer a course in philosophy at some point in your studies—whether required or elective.

A course in philosophy (which in Greek literally means "love of wisdom") will attempt to familiarize you with the Greek philosophers and how (Greek) philosophy in the early church greatly influenced later theology. After studying the Greek philosophers and early Greek Christians, the course might then explore important European philosophers like John

Locke or Søren Kierkegaard, or discuss more contemporary philosophy which interacts with issues related to postmodernity, truth, meaning, and culture in relation to the church.

Sample of Seminaries Offering Degrees related to (Systematic) Theology

Seminary	Degree
Moravian Theological Seminary (www.moravianseminary.edu)	Master of Arts in Theological Studies
University of Chicago Divinity School (http://divinity.uchicago.edu)	Master of Arts in Divinity Doctor of Philosophy in Theology
University of St. Thomas School of Theology (www.stthom.edu)	Master of Arts in Theological Studies
Vanderbilt University Divinity School (www.vanderbilt.edu/divinity)	Master of Theological Studies

In this chapter we have covered a good deal of territory. After explaining the common fourfold division of seminary courses, I isolated the first two—biblical studies and systematic theology—in depth. The next chapter will resume our discussion by focusing on the last two disciplines that seminaries offer: church history and practical theology.

12

Coursework and Classes

Church History and Practical Theology

This chapter will focus on the last two disciplines in seminary: church history and practical theology. Unlike biblical studies and systematic theology, for instance, these two disciplines have been traditionally less represented in the earliest seminaries. Of these two, practical theology is probably the more popular, and it is certainly more diverse. But I will let you in on a little secret: church history is perhaps the most interesting discipline of all. In this discipline you will meet the most fascinating, most overlooked, and certainly most unusual characters in all history. Whether you become a church historian or not, I hope this chapter will help you understand these disciplines.

Church History/Historical Theology

The third division of seminary curriculum—and the first one that we will discuss in this chapter—is church history. This discipline attempts to understand the development of the church's teachings via documents, events, and persons throughout history. Church history is further related to a discipline known as historical theology. The distinction between the two is in the stress of the name—the second name to be precise. Historical theologians stress theology within a historical context. Church historians, by contrast, emphasize history within an ecclesial or churchly context. A church historian, for example, is essentially a historian who works for the church. She is interested in, say, the social context or the political environment of eighteenth-century England during the time of John Wesley. A historical theologian is a theologian who looks at theology through the lens of history. He is interested in, say, how John Wesley's doctrine of sin developed throughout his life.

> 66 Labor to work yourself up into a temper correspondent with what you read, for that reading is useless which only enlightens the understanding without warming the affections. 99
>
> *John Wesley*

Classes in church history will provide similar services. They will isolate the fundamentals of the history of Christian doctrine as well as investigate the major events and personalities throughout the centuries. Here you will learn that Saint Augustine was no saint before he became a Christian! In church history you will also learn, for instance, that Thomas Aquinas's brothers supposedly locked him up in the family castle for two years to dissuade him from becoming a Dominican monk. (It didn't work.)

In a church history course you will also learn that the term *Methodist* was initially pejorative. John Wesley and his colleagues were called Methodists while at Oxford because they appeared to be too methodical, that is, fanatical in their study and embodiment of the Christian life. To accommodate all of these various facts and personalities at a typical seminary, the department of church history usually divides its curricula into two or three classes.

Early and Medieval Church History

The first church history course typically covers the period after the New Testament (roughly AD 100) up to the end of the Middle Ages (roughly AD 1500). You will examine the early heresies in the church, such as Arianism and Montanism, and you will spend some time working through the early councils at Nicaea, Constantinople, and so forth. During the medieval period you will study the development of the Catholic church, the papal system, scholasticism, and much more (remember to consult Appendix 3 for unfamiliar theological terms). Such notables as Peter Abelard (a French theologian) and Julian of Norwich (a British mystic) might enter the discussion. The first course will usually end toward the close of the medieval period and the beginning of the Reformation and Counter-Reformation.

Protestant Reformation and Modern Church History

This next church history course will usually begin at the Reformation (around 1500) and continue until the present. It will discuss such notables as Martin Luther, John Calvin, and Ignatius of Loyola, the separation of Protestantism from Catholicism, the rise of the modern state, and the Council of

Trent. Next comes the modern era in Europe, missions, colonization, and Christianity in the so-called third world. The rest of the course may then concentrate on the church in America, but each school stresses different themes. Some schools emphasize the Reformation or doctrinal issues, while others stress contemporary theology or something else. It all depends on the school and the professor.

American Church History (Required or Elective)

Because many of us live in the United States, it is only natural that some seminaries offer required courses in American church history (seminaries in Canada may offer courses on North American church history). Schools that do so usually divide the course into an exploration of the following: the early history of America and Puritanism, the first and second Great Awakenings, religion during the Civil War, the controversies between liberalism and fundamentalism, and the relations between church and state in the United States. Another aspect of the course might isolate famous American theologians such as Jonathan Edwards, Henry Ward Beecher, or Martin Luther King, Jr.

> 66 I advise no one to enter any religious order or the priesthood …unless he… understands that the works of monks and priests…do not differ one whit in the sight of God from the works of the rustic laborer in the field or the woman going about her household tasks. 99
>
> *Martin Luther*

Possible Course Division of Church History Curriculum in Seminary

Early, Medieval	AD 100–1500: Councils, Creeds, Middle Ages, Monasticism
Reformation, Modern	1500–Present: Protestantism, Rationalism, Postmodernism
American	1600–Present: Puritanism, Liberalism, and Fundamentalism

Sample of Seminaries Offering Degrees Related to Church History

Seminary	Degree
Gordon-Conwell Theological Seminary (www.gcts.edu)	Master of Arts in Church History Master of Theology in Church History
Grand Rapids Theological Seminary (http://grts.cornerstone.edu)	Master of Arts in Historical Theology
Princeton Theological Seminary (www.ptsem.edu)	Master of Theology in Church History Doctor of Philosophy in Church History
Westminster Seminary of California (www.wscal.edu)	Master of Arts in Historical Theology

Practical Theology

The discipline of practical theology is the last of the four divisions of seminary curriculum. As its name designates, it is practical in nature. There are many subdisciplines within the area of practical theology: (1) homiletics, (2) counseling, (3) (Christian) education, (4) evangelism, and (5) spirituality. (See the thirteenth and sixteenth chapters for discussions of topics related to music, worship, or liturgy.) These classes—while still requiring homework, papers, and tests like the other courses—are more interested in matters practical or ministerial than theoretical. In other words, you are required to use your heart just as much as your head. Practical classes are more introspective and concerned with making you a better person and minister. They teach you the skills that are needed primarily when working with a church: how to counsel, how to preach, how to preside over weddings and funerals, and how to relate particular Christian doctrines and beliefs to both yourself and the contemporary world around you. The following are the many different types of practical classes offered at seminary. Courses in practical theology are particularly helpful for those students interested in pastoral ministry and counseling.

Homiletics

Homiletics is the technical term for the study of preaching. Hence, homiletics or preaching seeks to make you a better speaker and teacher. You will study books written by professional preachers, be required to write papers with your reflections and thoughts, and actually preach a couple of sermons in front of class. These sermons are usually evaluated by your fellow students and your professor. Often, you will be videotaped when you preach. I thought that the homiletics course that I took while in seminary was extremely beneficial. It taught me not only how to speak in public confidently and successfully, but also a great deal about myself and how I relate to others. Even if you do not intend to preach regularly, you may want to consider taking a homiletics course sometime during your studies.

> Homiletics *is the technical term for the study of preaching.*

Counseling

These classes are designed to equip you with the necessary tools to counsel effectively. You will read books, learn different models of counseling, work on individual or group projects, and even perhaps be required to counsel someone for a grade. This is also usually a very helpful course, because it teaches you how to interact with people and how to help them. This is, in fact, the principal purpose of practically any ministry. Counseling courses will help you with any kind of relationship—whether marriage, friendship, or family. When I was in seminary, my wife audited a counseling course; she found it very useful.

There are various theories of counseling, and you will learn which are better than others and, more importantly, when or when not to use them. More and more these days, seminaries are requiring that every student be exposed to some type of counseling course. And there is good reason for doing so. No matter what you study in seminary, people are going to look to you as a person to whom they can come for advice. Because you are going to seminary, you will be regarded by many as an authority figure—as one who can be trusted and who can offer sound advice. The best preparation that I can think of is to take a class or two in counseling.

> 66 You will never prosper in your religious life in the Theological Seminary until your work in the Theological Seminary becomes itself to you a religious exercise out of which you draw every day enlargement of heart, elevation of spirit, and adoring delight in your Maker and your Savior. 99
>
> *B. B. Warfield*
> *(former professor at Princeton Seminary)*

Christian Education (Required or Elective)

Christian education encompasses the whole person with regard to learning and teaching. It is holistic in nature and construes the task of learning to be much more detailed than simply assimilating information. It considers the spiritual component to learning just as much as the intellectual. Although offered as an elective at practically every seminary, it is sometimes a required course. If you do take a course in Christian education, you will most likely consider the following themes: how individuals learn, the difference between Christian education and secular education, strategies for teaching effectively, and different methods employed when teaching and learning.

Evangelism/Missions (Required or Elective)

Evangelism, or missions, is an area of practical theology that teaches you how to share your beliefs with other people and how to help improve the social conditions of others around you. These classes introduce you to the biblical teaching on evangelism, famous missionaries of the past, and what your role is as an evangelist and worker of Christ. Books on evangelism and culture will be studied, with the usual tests and papers being mandatory as well. There will also most likely be practical components to evangelism. I once took a class, for instance, where the professor required each student to share his or her faith with thirteen different non-Christians—with the complete account written in a journal—over one semester. I never worked so hard in my life! Although this exercise was probably excessive, it helped us realize how important it is for Christians to share our faith, embody our beliefs, and serve our neighbors.

Classes on missions are similar to classes on evangelism, but they are usually oriented more pointedly toward culture and sociology.

Classes on evangelism or missions traditionally have been considered together. Today, however, the concept of mission (singular) has become a very popular discipline in its own right.

They will teach you how to prepare for a career in the mission field, whether locally or abroad. You will learn different approaches (theories) to missions, and how to interact with local residents, be transparent, incarnate the gospel, and deal with the specific issues that are raised on the mission field. For example, you might learn what to do if you move to a culture where polygamy is openly tolerated (a concern for some Western missionaries in the past who worked in parts of Africa). You will also learn how to plant churches, maintain church growth, and be culturally sensitive and relevant, and how best to offer physical and spiritual relief to areas of need. You may even learn how to supervise working projects, how to build homes for those in need, and how you can improve the living conditions of those to whom you minister.

Spirituality (Elective)

Classes on spirituality are almost contradictory. How can anyone grade whether you are a spiritual person or, worse, spiritual enough to pass a course? These courses focus on an area that ironically receives little attention in seminary. In courses related to this discipline, you will read books on spirituality and be involved in several projects related to the spiritual life.

You will consider, for instance, your spiritual gifts—whether in teaching, praying, serving, giving, or receiving. You will also look at spiritual disciplines, which are the different disciplines that Christians have practiced through the centuries to help them relate better to God and others. Spiritual disciplines are practices such as prayer, meditation, charity, generosity, and fasting. A class on spirituality will also teach you how to cultivate a spirit-led life, how to enrich other people's lives spiritually, and how to be a better Christian. The last aspect of a course on spirituality might be dedicated to studying various individuals in church history who were known for their spirituality. These figures are often monks and nuns like

St. Benedict (an early Italian saint), Bernard of Clairvaux (medieval French monk), and St. Teresa of Avila (sixteenth-century Spanish nun), who have greatly influenced the church over the centuries through their writings and spiritual exercises.

Possible Course Division of Practical Theology Curriculum in Seminary

Homiletics	Understanding How to Preach and Teach Effectively
Counseling	Learning Specific Techniques, Gaining Experiences as a Counselor
Education	Integrating Faith and Learning; Holistic Education
Evangelism	Sharing Faith with Others, Organizing Events, Empowering Others, Building Relationships
Spirituality	Spiritual Disciplines: Prayer, Giving, Humility, Bible Reading, Loving

Sample of Seminaries Offering Degrees Related to Practical Theology

Seminary	Degree
Associated Mennonite Biblical Seminary (www.ambs.edu)	Master of Arts in Christian Formation Master of Arts in Mission and Evangelism
George Fox Evangelical Seminary (www.georgefox.edu/seminary)	Master of Arts in Spiritual Formation Doctor of Ministry (Leadership and Spiritual Formation)
Lutheran Theological Seminary at Gettysburg (www.ltsg.edu)	Master of Arts in Ministry
Seventh-day Adventist Theological Seminary (www.andrews.edu/SEM)	Master of Arts in Pastoral Ministry Master of Arts in Religious Education

Field or Ministry Experience

There is in addition to taking classes another very important aspect to seminary curricula that relates mostly to practical theology courses: field experience or mentored ministry. The truth is that most seminaries require some type of field experience—depending, of course, on the program and specific school. This practical knowledge can be learned in many different arenas. It can be learned in the local church, a missions trip, a counseling office, a hospital, a Christian organization, and so forth. This experiential component of seminary is intended to give you practical exposure to ministry, so that you will be qualified professionally upon graduating.

Historically, the first seminaries in the United States did not include this subject as part of their curricula, but eventually it caught on. Perhaps one of the most desirable changes needed in seminary education today relates to the need for more practical learning. Many seminary graduates, unfortunately, are poorly prepared for the practical issues they soon encounter in ministry: dealing with division, hurt, dishonesty, abuse, and the politics of Christian ministry. Many seminaries are now correcting this.

Naturally, some seminaries do better than others. Although there are some that do not mandate field experience, every seminary recommends it. Many seminaries require from their students some form of practical experience in order to graduate. I know of a denominational seminary where all ministerial candidates are required to have one full year of ministry experience before they can be ordained. Usually, students complete this year-long experience after their second year of seminary. Subsequent to their internships, they typically come back for their last year of education energized, experienced, and confident that they had learned a great deal about the ministry.

Clinical Pastoral Education (CPE)

If your particular school does not offer mandatory field experience for graduation, you should try to get some experience anyway, whether during the summer, concurrently with school, or by taking off a semester from coursework and working at a church or other organization. Many denominations require what is referred to as clinical pastoral education (CPE). This is a required internship, which can be fulfilled during the summer between semesters. It provides practical experience in the fields of counseling and leadership. You will most likely work at a hospital or similar setting for the entire summer as an intern. There you will encounter real-life situations and hardships that will challenge what you have been learning in your more theoretical classes. Such training is highly valuable upon entering your profession full time, because it introduces you to the kinds of problems that you will most likely be dealing with on a regular basis if you enter the pastorate or a similar position.

Clinical pastoral education (CPE) refers to an internship that many denominations require for students who want to be ordained. It often takes place in hospitals.

Summary of Seminary Curriculum

By now you have probably realized that seminary is work. There are numerous courses that you will be required to take in various disciplines during your theological training. But as I stated at the beginning of the last chapter, every seminary and program is different. Perhaps you are interested solely in counseling or church history. Do you still have to take all these courses? It depends. If you intend to enroll in the classic degree—the master of divinity—you will certainly have to take courses in all of these disciplines. If it is your professional objective to become a counselor, however, you probably will not be required to take classes in, say, the biblical languages or similar subjects. However, all seminarians—regardless of degree—are required to take certain courses, for instance, in biblical studies and theology. Seminaries are very similar to colleges in this respect, as they both entail a variety of required courses. For example, regardless of your college major, you probably had to take at least a semester or two of a foreign language or mathematics. Seminary will likewise require certain courses. Which ones? Are there any alternatives? What are the options when it comes to classes and specific programs? Good questions! These are the very topics and questions that we will consider in the next two chapters about seminary degrees and programs.

13

Different Degrees of Seminary

Basic Programs

Have you ever wondered when seminary degrees came into being? They were first offered after the Civil War in the United States—when urban life was supplanting rural life. At this time seminaries had been in existence in America for less than a hundred years, and they were on the rise. By the twentieth century, they had become professionalized and standardized. The typical seminary degree, the master of divinity, was then called the "bachelor of divinity." Yale Divinity School, for instance, first offered the bachelor of divinity in 1867; a century later they changed the name to the master of divinity, as most every other seminary in North America has done.

Different Degrees and Programs

In the previous two chapters we learned about the fourfold division of seminary curricula as well as the types of courses that you will most likely take. This discussion of coursework and classes naturally directs our attention to the next sequence of seminary education: discovering the different degrees that seminaries offer. The next two chapters will look at the many degree possibilities at seminary, so that you can discover the program that is best suited for you.

In contrast to seminary education several decades ago, seminaries today offer a variety of programs. You can find a degree in practically any field of interest. For the most part, larger schools offer more unique or special-ized degrees—mostly because of funding, resources, and more specialized personnel. Southwestern Baptist Theological Seminary (www.swbts.edu) in Fort Worth, for example, offers several distinctive and in-novative programs as a result of its great size and specialized faculty and staff. One of these distinct programs is a Master of Arts in Islamic Culture, which is a degree designed for missionaries to Muslim countries. If you are looking for a degree this specialized, you should be aware that you will most likely have to move—usually out of state. If, however, you simply want to enroll in the classic degree at seminary, the master of divinity, you will have few problems: virtually every seminary in North America offers it.

The classic seminary degree is the master of divinity. Virtually every seminary offers it.

Basic or First-Professional Programs versus Advanced or Graduate Programs

Let us begin our discussion by looking at the differences between basic and advanced programs. In the second chapter of this book, we talked about how seminaries are professional (graduate) schools like law schools and medical schools. They are called professional schools because each of these schools prepares students for specific professions upon graduation: lawyers, doctors, or ministers. In addition to being professional schools, however, seminaries are considered graduate institutions. This is because professional schools require an undergraduate degree from college—since professional schools typically provide only graduate or postbaccalaureate degrees for students. In this context, seminaries usually offer only master's and doctoral degrees—not bachelor's degrees. However, these different types of programs vary considerably. Some are called basic programs. Essentially, basic programs are first theological de-grees. If you have never attended seminary before, you are eligible only for a basic degree. The other kinds of programs that seminaries offer are advanced or graduate programs. These can be pursued only after a basic degree has been earned. All doctoral degrees are advanced degrees; a master's degree can be either a basic or an advanced degree (though it is almost always a basic degree). Are you confused yet? You will learn about these differences below!

Basic or First-Professional Degree Programs

Generally speaking, the majority of students at seminary will be en-rolled in what are considered basic degrees or first-professional degrees.

These programs prepare you for a particular profession: becoming a pastor, counselor, educator, missionary, layperson, and so forth. They are the most common and popular degrees, and the majority of students will be enrolled in one of these programs. Seminaries usually classify basic degrees into one of two categories.

Types of Basic Degrees:

Master of divinity

Master of arts (many varieties)

Master of theological studies

For the most part, basic degrees are classified into (1) ministerial degrees or (2) academic degrees. Ministerial basic degrees focus on practical ministry, while academic basic degrees focus on academic training. In a word, if you want to become a pastor, you will probably enroll in a basic ministerial degree; by contrast, if you want to become a teacher or professor, you will probably want to enroll in a basic academic degree. Although seminaries do make such distinctions, there is a good deal of overlap between the two degrees. And of course there are countless students who fall somewhere in between wanting to become pastors and wanting to become professors.

Two Kinds of Basic Programs

Ministerial—More ministry-related (counseling, missions, and so on)

Academic—More research-related (biblical studies, theology, and so on)

Advanced or Graduate Degree Programs (Preview for Next Chapter)

Upon graduating from seminary with a basic degree, certain students—due to their vocational objectives—may be in need of additional education. This is particularly the case for students who desire to teach at the college or seminary level, or for those who want to improve their effectiveness as a pastor or missionary. If this describes your situation, there are essentially two different types of programs: an advanced master's degree or a variety of doctoral degrees. These degrees are considered graduate degrees because they require a previous master's degree from seminary—a basic degree. As is the case at other schools and universities, every degree is dependent upon an earlier degree. A master's degree at a secular university, in other words, is dependent on a bachelor's degree, just as a doctorate at seminary is dependent upon a previous master's degree there.

Types of Advanced Degrees

Master of Theology (ThM, MTh, STM)

Doctor of Ministry (DMin)

Doctor of Missiology (DMiss)

Doctor of Musical Arts (DMA)

Doctor of Education (EdD)

Doctor of Clinical Psychology (PsyD)

Doctor of Philosophy (PhD)

Doctor of Sacred Theology (STD)

Doctor of Theology (ThD)

Variety of Basic or First-Professional Degrees Offered

The only programs that we will consider in this chapter are what we earlier called basic degrees. As I explained above, these are the primary degrees offered at seminary. Included is the classic seminary degree—the master of divinity—as well as other closely related degrees that are referred to in several ways: master of arts, master of theological studies, and even the master of religion. In contrast to the master of divinity, each of these three degrees refers to programs with similar objectives. For this reason, below I will subsume each of them under the sole category of the master of arts.

If you want to eventually enroll in a graduate program while in seminary, you will probably need to earn the master of divinity as your basic degree.

Generally speaking, the master of divinity is the preferred degree for students pursuing ordination or another related form of ministry while the master of arts (and therefore the master of theological studies and the master of religion) is the preferred degree for students who are not intending to become ordained. However, if you are not certain whether you are called to pastoral (ordained) ministry, it may be recommended to enroll in the master of divinity. This is because it is the standard degree that will serve as the foundation to any career in the ministry.

Master of Divinity (MDiv)

Master of Divinity

Three to four years full time

Both academic and ministerial

For any ministry (traditionally pastoral)

General focus (sometimes specific)

The MDiv is the bread-and-butter of theological education. This standard seminary degree is normally completed full time in around three or four years—roughly one hundred credits or more, which is two to three times as long as the typical master's degree at a university! It is a smorgasbord of theological learning. You will take courses in biblical studies (possibly the biblical languages), systematic theology, church history, and practical theology, as well as field education or internships. This degree will prepare you for any avenue of Christian ministry you might eventually pursue. It is the degree typically needed for ordination, and the one usually required for further graduate degrees at seminary.

Master of Arts

Two or three years full time

Academic or ministerial (not both)

Not for pastoral ministry (ordination)

Specialization (in one specific area)

Historically, the master of divinity (as it is called today at least) was the most popular degree that seminaries offered. This made complete sense then because most seminarians pursued ordination and pastoral ministry for the remainder of their careers. The few that did not pursue this avenue of ministry typically entered academia or the mission field. Since that time, however, seminary education has evolved considerably. Fewer and fewer seminarians enter the pastoral life. They are interested instead in any number of other professional careers. This trend in seminary education may or may not reflect your specific vision for ministry. If it does, do not feel pressured to pursue the master of divinity just because it is the "typical" degree. Rather, you should enter another master's degree that is related to your field of interest. But if you are not certain what you will do upon graduation, it is generally recommended that you enroll in the master of divinity while in seminary.

If you have no idea what you want to do after graduating but know that you are called to go to seminary, complete the master of divinity.

Master of Divinity Students Are Classified as Follows

First year—Junior

Second year—Middler

Third year—Senior

Career Prospects for Those Who Graduate with the Master of Divinity

- Pastoral ministry (ordination or not)
- Missions, church planting, evangelism, preaching
- Teaching, education (church, secondary, college, or seminary)
- Staff member at a Christian organization (parachurch, related institution)
- Miscellaneous (this degree serves as the foundation for countless other careers)

Concentrations in the Master of Divinity

Above I described the master of divinity as a smorgasbord of theological education. This is because the master of divinity offers courses in a variety of subjects related to theology—from church history to preaching. Although it is correct to characterize the master of divinity as being general in focus, there are many seminaries these days that allow students to additionally specialize in a specific discipline of their interest. Typically, these concentrations are in such fields as pastoral ministry, counseling, general studies, or an area such as biblical studies or church history. Some seminaries even provide more specific concentrations. Bethel Theological Seminary (http://seminary.bethel.edu) in St. Paul, for instance, provides a concentration in marriage and family studies for students who need training in family ministries. Additionally, Multnomah Biblical Seminary (www.multnomah.edu/seminary) in Portland, Oregon, offers a concentration in hospital chaplaincy for those in the master of divinity program who are called to be chaplains. These two schools illustrate that the master of divinity offered at many seminaries—though general in focus—does allow for specialized instruction in other theological areas of interest.

Although the master of divinity degree is traditionally very general, many schools these days allow for concentrations.

Joint or Dual Master of Divinity

In addition to the traditional master of divinity there is also what is called a "joint" or "dual" master of divinity. It is so called because the master of divinity is obtained in conjunction with another degree. Both these degrees are pursued concurrently. This option has become increasingly popular over the years, particularly with the need for more advanced specialization in professional fields these days. Typically, the degree that is not the master of divinity is pursued in a different school within the larger university or seminary. At other times two separate schools (a seminary and a university) collaborate so that the seminary offers the master of divinity while the university offers the other degree. This other degree is usually not a degree in theology or divinity.

Regent University (www.regent.edu/acad/schdiv/) in Virginia Beach, for instance, offers a joint master of divinity and juris doctor (law degree) for students. Although the student receives both degrees from the university, different schools within the university offer the individual classes: students take classes for the master of divinity at the divinity school, while they take classes for the juris doctor at the law school.

The "joint" master of divinity is a program which leads to two separate degrees: the master of divinity and another professional degree, which is not related to theology.

Similarly, Wake Forest University (http://divinity/wfu.edu) in Winston-Salem, North Carolina, offers a dual degree in divinity and counseling. This is a program intended for those who are in need of specialized training in both theology and counseling services. Through the course of four years, students take classes at the divinity school and in the department of counseling. After successful completion of coursework, students are awarded both the master of divinity and the master of arts in counseling.

There are several additional joint master of divinity programs across the country. These are excellent programs for those who desire more detailed training, because they compress the time required for degrees that would otherwise be sought individually. However, because students are enrolled in two degrees simultaneously, these programs usually take at least four years to complete and are therefore expensive. Moreover, it is important to note that when applying for the joint master of divinity, students must be admitted into both degree programs separately. You must be admitted to the master of divinity from seminary in addition to the degree from the cooperating school.

Possible Sequence for Master of Divinity in Seminary

Biblical	Old and New Testaments; Greek and Hebrew	21–30 Credits
Theological	Systematic Theology; Ethics	18–24 Credits
Historical	Church History	6–9 Credits
Practical	Counseling; Education; Evangelism; Homiletics	15–21 Credits
Electives	Elective classes	12–18 Credits
Internship	Field ministry experience	6–12 Credits
Total	All classes and requirements	90–120 Credits

Master of Arts (MA)

The master of arts is usually a two- or three-year degree—when done full time—of roughly forty to sixty credits. It is a year shorter than the classic master of divinity coursework. The master of arts is designed primarily for those who are not interested in becoming a pastor of a church and hence are not seeking ordination. In this respect, it is not unlike the type of degree that could be earned at a graduate school of religion. Today, the master of arts is as diverse as the size and shape of each seminary. It requires a particular specialty that will enable the graduate to excel in his or her field. A dissertation may or may not be required (depending on how academic or ministerial the program is). Generally speaking, more ministerial programs will not require a dissertation, while more academic programs may or may not.

ACADEMIC/GENERAL THEOLOGY PROGRAMS FOR THE MASTER OF ARTS

The master of arts can be an academic or theological degree, on the one hand, or a more ministerial or practical degree, on the other. For those who pursue a more academic or theological program, this degree would suffice as entrance into a PhD program, but not a doctor of ministry—since a PhD is purely academic, whereas a doctor of ministry is, by and large, ministerial or practical in nature.

A more academically focused master of arts is typically earned by students who want to enter careers related to teaching and research. You should pursue this type of program, for instance, if you know for certain that you want to eventually pursue a PhD and therefore do not require the practical or ministerial courses offered in the master of divinity (which will add an extra year). Just make sure that you specialize in the area that you intend to specialize in for a PhD. In other words, if you would ultimately like to enroll in a PhD in systematic theology, it is important that you first obtain an MA in (systematic) theology. For those who want to eventually enroll in a PhD program, there are generally two options available for you upon obtaining a master's degree from seminary: the first option is to enroll in a doctoral program at a secular university, while the second is to do so at a seminary. In the main, university doctoral programs prefer the master of arts while seminary doctoral programs prefer the master of divinity. When all is said and done, however, students are admitted into doctoral programs with either basic degree.

Students who are interested in a dual degree must apply and be admitted into both the divinity school and the other professional school.

Two Alternatives for Those Interested in a PhD

Earn the master of arts for university teaching.

Earn the master of divinity for seminary teaching.

MINISTERIAL OR PRACTICAL PROGRAMS FOR THE MASTER OF ARTS

By discussing PhD options with you I do not mean to imply that the master of arts is only for those who want to obtain doctorates in the future. The master of arts is extremely diverse. It is currently becoming the most pragmatic degree for many students—particularly as a result of the increasing number of students attending seminary for reasons other than eventual ordination. The degree is accordingly being pursued by more students than ever before who have interest in neither academia nor Christian ministry per se. Instead, they are pursuing other professional careers. Still other students enrolled in the master of arts degree desire to enter the ministry but do not seek ordination.

Types of Master's Degrees

Although the most common designation for this degree is master of arts, many seminaries refer to it by a different name. As I stated above, certain schools refer to this degree as a master of theological studies (MTS) or a master of religion (MAR), or in a similar way. However, for the most part, each of these degrees is essentially the same. Specifically, they are basic seminary degrees that prepare students for a particular specialization in theology other than pastoral ministry. For this reason, I will confine myself mostly to the most common name these degrees go by, the master of arts. Below we will discuss many—but not all—of the particular specializations students can pursue under the master of arts. Although I distinguished the academic or theological programs from the ministerial/professional ones above, I will discontinue this use below. This is because your seminary degree will show no such distinction, nor will most anyone else distinguish the two. I will instead distinguish the programs by area of concentration.

The master of arts is not just for future scholars. It's a common degree for students with many interests.

MA in Biblical Studies

The degree in biblical studies is designed either for students who want to pursue a PhD in biblical studies or for those who want to increase their understanding of the biblical texts and languages without studying for the master of divinity. It is usually divided into a deeper specialization in either the Old or New Testament. You will most likely study and translate the biblical languages (Hebrew and/or Greek). This usually entails two or three courses in your biblical area of choice. The program also seeks to give you the tools necessary to: translate the biblical text, understand it historically and culturally, discern the larger narrative of the Bible, and learn how to research and write. You will write several exegesis papers and possibly a short dissertation on a particular issue within biblical studies. This program is mostly academic and contains many of the same classes found in the master of divinity—save the ministerial courses. By the time you graduate, you should be informed of all the major aspects within your field and equipped to handle the biblical text responsibly and confidently.

Possible Career Options

Eventually enter a PhD program in biblical studies

Become a Bible teacher (at church, high school)

MA in (Christian) Education or Religious Education

This degree is ideal for Christian educators, either at the primary or the secondary level. The goal is integrating faith and learning. You will take several courses in educational or psychological theory, and general classes about theology as well as the Bible. You will additionally supervise several projects designed to help you become a better educator. This program does not generally enable you to pass state examinations for certification, because most recipients of this degree will work in Christian schools that will not necessarily require certification (see the fifteenth chapter for licensure information).

This degree is thus not recommended for Christians who desire to teach at secular schools. If this describes your situation, you should probably attend a Christian college or university and complete your master's in education there—which will most likely prepare you for state certification. The master of arts in Christian education is perhaps better suited for teachers who want to become more informed about education and theology, and it is certainly the most appropriate degree for teachers in churches—whether as a teaching or education minister, Sunday school teacher, or nursery coordinator.

Possible Career Options

Educator at church

Schoolteacher (secondary education)

Professor (after earning doctorate)

MA in Church History/Historical Theology

Are you fascinated with the *when*, *where*, and *who* of church history? If so, you may be a perfect candidate for the master of arts in church history. In this program you will learn all you would ever want to know about the history of the church. For this degree you will not merely specialize in church history; rather, you will also have to specialize further in the early, medieval, Reformation, or modern church. You will primarily study church history, but you will also take courses in other areas: biblical studies, theology, and perhaps Latin or Greek. This degree is usually sufficient for entrance into a PhD in church history, theology, or religion. It is also appropriate for those who want to teach church history or theology at the secondary-school level. The program in church history is effectively academic and contains many of the same classes found in the master of divinity—excluding the ministerial classes, of course. A dissertation may be required.

MA in (Christian) Counseling/Marriage and Family Therapy/ Psychology

Students who desire to be counselors, therapists, or eventually (clinical) psychologists are advised to enroll in this program. It matters little in the beginning whether you are interested in working at the local church, in private practice, in preparation for a doctorate in counseling or clinical psychology, or at a Christian clinic. In this respect, the program is extremely diverse. It is also a suitable degree for adults interested in counseling who will use the skills learned in the program to help their church or future ministry context. You will take courses in counseling, psychology, and practical theology, as well as general classes in biblical studies and theology. If you are pursuing state certification as a counselor or therapist, you should check with your seminary of interest (see the fifteenth chapter for more information about licensure).

If you want to become a counselor, you should decide early on whether you want to be licensed.

Some schools work closely with the state toward certification, while others do not. Furthermore, some programs include thorough practical and online experience. With this degree in particular, make sure that you are familiar and in accord with the goals of the program before you enter, so as not to waste time and money. Some—but not all—schools have tracks for those seeking certification and are thus excellent alternatives to secular universities.

Possible Career Options

Counselor (licensed or not)

Clinical psychologist

Therapist

Church worker

Counseling professor at college or seminary (after earning doctorate)

MA in Leadership

Interest in leadership has grown over the past several years to the extent that there are currently several seminaries that offer related programs. Programs that specialize in leadership are typically distinct from the master of divinity, which means that they are programs intentionally designed for students who will not enter pastoral ministry. Career prospects for those who obtain this degree are varied: leadership or administration at a Christian organization, educated layperson, or leading at the church or the secular level.

MA in Ministry/Practical Theology

The degree in ministry or practical theology is applicable to those involved in practical ministry—whether as a worker at a Christian clinic, at a parachurch organization, as a social worker, as an assistant minister at a local church, or simply as an informed layperson. The degree is ministerial in nature, which means that you will take courses concerned with counseling, discipleship, Christian living, evangelism, and so forth. However, you will also take some academic courses, such as biblical studies or theology.

Possible Career Options

Worker at church, parachurch, or other Christian institution

Layperson

This degree is perhaps the best option for those interested in receiving a seminary education without wanting to make a career change—in other words, for the informed layperson. If you are content with your career but would like to offer your services to the church in your free time as an elder, a deacon, or a teacher, this degree just might be what you are looking for. However, this degree is also capable of preparing full-time Christian workers for ministry. I have a friend, for instance, who completed this degree not knowing what to expect professionally upon graduation. She is currently serving with her husband as a full-time domestic missionary.

MA in Missions/Missiology/Cross-Cultural Ministries/Evangelism

Do you love traveling to new places? Do you love people? Then maybe you should consider a degree in missions or evangelism. It will prepare you for the mission field—whether abroad in remote lands or in your own country. You will take courses in sociology, culture, evangelism, theology, and biblical studies, and perhaps courses about languages and translation. The program should also enable you to find that particular region of the world where you are called to minister. Keep in mind, however, that graduating from this program does not mean that they send you off on the mission field the day you graduate! The program simply prepares you for that profession, and it provides a network of friends toward that endeavor. Enrollment in this program will also expose you to various missionary organizations and other professionals that should be able to direct you to your area of effectiveness. A degree in evangelism usually differs from one in missions, but not extensively.

MA in Music (Worship)/Master of Church Music/ Master of Sacred Music

Music has always been important to the church. In fact, Pope Gregory the Great founded the first Christian music school in Rome (during the sixth century), in order to preserve Christian music for future generations. Today there are currently more jobs available for Christian musicians than has ever been the case. If you want to lead worship without necessarily leading the church through preaching or administering the sacraments, a degree in music might be the perfect option for you.

Possible Career Options

Worship leader at church

Music education (secondary Christian school)

Professor of music (after earning doctorate)

Independent musician

There are several different types of degrees related to music, which differ according to specific career objectives and the focus of the school.

For the most part, these degrees are ideal for ministers of music at local churches, music teachers at a primary or secondary Christian school, choir directors, organists, pianists, vocalists, and even future college and seminary professors in music. You will take courses in music composition, theory, and history, as well as general classes in theology and biblical studies. You may have the opportunity to specialize in whatever area of music interests you, whether composition, education, history, theory, worship, organ, piano, or vocal.

MA in (Systematic) Theology

This is intended for students who desire thorough exposure to theology. You may have to specialize further in either systematic theology or historical theology. You will primarily study theology, but you will also take courses in other areas: biblical studies, perhaps the biblical languages, church history, and so forth. This degree is usually sufficient for entrance into a PhD in theology or religion. Accordingly, it is essentially academic. A dissertation therefore may be required. In this program you will write several papers about theological concepts and issues in theology, and specific doctrines throughout church history.

Possible Career Options

Eventually enroll in PhD program in theology

Teach at secondary-school level

Work at church as teaching minister

MA in . . .

Seminaries in the twenty-first century offer degrees of many kinds. In fact, each decade brings with it innovations in seminary curriculum that offer new and very specialized programs. It is impossible therefore to describe in detail every concentration or specific program in the master of arts. There are literally dozens of other concentrations that seminaries offer that I have not described above. Southeastern Baptist Theological Seminary (www.sebts.edu) in Wake Forest, North Carolina, for instance, offers two such innovative concentrations for the master of arts: a concentration in women's studies as well as Christian school administration. If you are interested in seminary but not necessarily in one of the areas that I discussed above, I encourage you to navigate the websites or request brochures from various seminaries that you are interested in attending.

Other Possible Master of Arts Programs at Seminaries

- Master of Arts in Family Ministries
- Master of Arts in Intercultural Studies/Ministries
- Master of Arts in Media or Communications
- Master of Arts in Pastoral Ministry/Studies
- Master of Arts in Religion
- Master of Arts in Spirituality
- Master of Arts in Urban Ministry
- Master of Arts in Youth Ministry

Possible Sequence for Master of Arts in Seminary

Biblical	Old and New Testaments	12–16 Credits
Theological	Systematic theology, ethics, church history	9–12 Credits
Elective	Elective classes	6 Credits
Specialization	Classes of specialization	12–15 Credits
Total	All classes and requirements	40–60 Credits

Certificate for Studies in Seminary

There is, in addition to the master of arts and master of divinity, another program offered at certain seminaries for entering students. It is not a degree, but a certificate. This program is designed for people who want to enhance their understanding of theology and ministry without changing their careers. Students in this program usually take several courses of their choosing and upon completion receive a certificate that they have completed a certain number of classes from seminary. This is perhaps the best alternative for those who want to better serve their churches but are not called into professional ministry, that is, for those who want to remain laypersons.

Possible Sequence for Certificate (of Theological Studies) in Seminary

Coursework	Three to seven courses
Specialty	Specific courses at student's discretion

Moving up a Degree

A certificate from seminary is a great way for a layperson to learn about theology without changing his or her career or spending too much time or money on seminary.

This chapter has, hopefully, helped you think through what type of degree and program you would like to pursue during seminary. There is certainly a good deal of variety when it comes to deciding on a program that suits you, and I pray that you will be directed to the right one along the way. The next chapter will focus on advanced degrees, that is, those degrees that require basic degrees for admission. If it so happens that upon receiving a basic degree you should find yourself either bold or bored, turn the page and see what dreams may come with an advanced degree from seminary!

14

Different Degrees of Seminary

Advanced Programs

The degrees described in the previous chapter are all basic or first-professional degrees. Therefore, they are the first degrees that students earn at seminary. If, however, graduates of these basic degrees seek further specialization in their areas of interest, they will do so under the auspices of an advanced or graduate degree. These are degrees in which a first-professional seminary degree—most always the master of divinity—is required for admission. Each of these programs normally requires writing a lengthy and original dissertation (or project) prior to graduating and is more in-depth and extensive than is the master of divinity. Advanced degrees also require specialization and more detailed mastery of a particular area within the field of ministry and theology. As stated above with regard to basic degrees, advanced degrees can be further divided into ministerial degrees or academic degrees.

Master of Theology (ThM or MTh)/Master of Sacred Theology (STM)

This degree is not to be confused with the basic programs such as the master of arts in theology (MA in theology) or the master of theological studies (MATS). However, the master of theology (ThM) is roughly synonymous with the master of sacred theology (STM), which was the traditional terminology for the degree. At most seminaries this degree will be referred to as either the STM or ThM. The distinction is slight: the STM may reflect a more ministerial focus, whereas the ThM may reflect a more research or academic focus. However, these distinctions are not exact.

The master of theology requires the master of divinity (or, very rarely, the master of arts). It is normally completed in one year full time or perhaps two or three years part time—depending also on whether you select the option of writing a dissertation or of taking more coursework. It requires specialization in a particular area—whether biblical studies, church history, spirituality, systematic theology, practical theology, homiletics, or another related discipline.

> **❝**If all the world were Christian, it might not matter if all the world were uneducated. But, as it is, a cultural life will exist outside the Church whether it exists inside or not. To be ignorant and simple now . . . would be to throw down our weapons, and to betray our uneducated brethren who have, under God, no defence but us against the intellectual attacks of the heathen. . . . The learned life then is, for some, a duty.**❞**
>
> *C. S. Lewis*
> *(Christian author*
> *and scholar)*

Possible Career Options

Continue at present job

Prepare for doctorate

Remain or become pastor, missionary, or teacher at church or school

The master of theology is designed for those who desire a deeper academic and ministerial exposure to theology without having to go full-fledged into a doctorate (which is both rigorous and expensive). It is a way for a full-time pastor or other seminary graduate to stay sharp theologically or to make further preparation for advanced study. Historically, this was the standard degree en route to a doctorate. With the advent of the doctor of ministry as well as the success of the doctor of philosophy, however, the master of theology has waned in popularity, and certain seminaries have removed it from their curriculum. But other schools maintain a high enrollment for this degree, since it is frequently considered a springboard for admittance into a PhD program. If you seek this degree, make sure to check with the seminary to ensure that it is appropriate or even available.

Possible Sequence for Master of Theology in Seminary

Prerequisite	Master of divinity
Languages	Competence in one or two foreign languages
Coursework	Seven to ten courses in area of specialty
Thesis (optional)	100–150 pages
Total Years	One to three

Doctor of Ministry (DMin)

Perhaps the most practical advanced degree that seminaries offer is the doctor of ministry. This degree is fairly recent, first penetrating seminary curriculum in the 1960s. It is intended for full-time ministers, missionaries, or those seeking to become professors in practical theology at a college or a seminary. The doctor of ministry is a popular degree for pastors who want to remain aware of the shifts of culture and of the latest theological trends, and for those who require more specialized training in an area related to their present or future career. More and more pastors these days are pursuing this degree, as it is both flexible and applicable to ministry.

You will take classes in preaching, counseling, contemporary culture, spirituality, and so forth. It is completed on a part-time basis (while you work full time in the ministry) and requires both the master of divinity and at least three years of full-time ministry after graduating from seminary. One of the great features of this degree is that it is pursued over a number of years—usually in classes that are offered a week at a time or in a similarly concentrated period. The degree, as a result, can be obtained by individuals living out of the area, out of the state, or even out of the country on occasion. It is very flexible and seeks to accommodate a student's full-time ministry.

The doctor of ministry typically requires a master of divinity and a few years of ministry experience for admittance. It is a ministerial (not academic) degree.

Although a doctorate in name, this degree is practical in nature and designed for those in real-life (not academic) ministry. It does, however, require a written project on a topic related to your area of ministry: church life, missions, culture and Christianity, and so on. If you want to teach a form of academic theology (such as biblical studies or church history), you need to enroll for a PhD and not a doctor of ministry. The doctor of ministry is ideal for the full-time pastor who really enjoyed seminary and wants to continue his or her education without entering a more academic program.

Possible Sequence for Doctor of Ministry in Seminary

Prerequisites	Master of divinity; full-time ministry experience
Coursework	Several modular courses in area of specialty
Ministerial component	Full-time ministry experience while in school
Final project	Final written project integrating area of specialty
Total years	Three to five years

Other Professional Doctoral Programs (Education, Missiology, Musical Arts)

There are in addition to the doctor of ministry several other degrees at seminary that are similar in nature to the doctor of ministry, but different in content. These degrees are variously labeled. What they have in common is their unique approach to graduate theological education. Each of these degrees represents the highest degree one can earn in his or her field but contrasts with the PhD by its commitment to more ministerial areas. Whereas the PhD, in other words, is mostly or completely academic, the following degrees are both academic and ministerial or practical.

Possible Career Options

Seminary or university professor

Researcher or independent academic

Administration at institution or other Christian organization

In this respect, they are very similar to the master of divinity—except that they are advanced and not basic degrees. One might say that these degrees are academically between the doctor of ministry and the doctor of philosophy. In this section we will highlight the important features of these degrees, but we will do so only briefly, since they are related to the discussions about the doctor of ministry and the PhD. Most of these degrees are designed for those who would like to teach at the college or seminary level; or for those who want to become practitioners in a Christian clinic or organization. Furthermore, they are usually offered only at select seminaries.

Most of these degrees are designed for those who would like to teach at the college or seminary level

- **Doctor of Education (EdD)**—Certain seminaries offer a doctor of education. This degree is intended primarily for those who want to teach (Christian) education at the college or seminary level, or for those in administration.
- **Doctor of Missiology (DMiss)**—A missiologist is an academic who studies trends and issues related to (Christian) missions. This degree is advisable only for those who want to become academics and seminary professors.

- **Doctor of Musical Arts (DMA)**—This program is ideal for those who will teach music at the college or seminary level.
- **Doctor of Psychology (PsyD)**—This very rare program at seminary prepares students for careers in clinical psychology and related services.

Possible Sequence for Related Doctoral Degrees in Seminary

Prerequisites	Master of divinity; ministerial experience
Coursework	Many courses in area of specialty
Practical components	Perhaps field ministry/interning
Written project	Writing a lengthy evaluative or research project
Total years	Four to six years

Doctor of Theology (ThD)

In the early part of the twentieth century, many of the seminaries that offered doctorates called them doctorates in theology. Over the years, however, most seminaries have converted to the terminology of PhD (doctor of philosophy). However, certain (very few) schools maintain the terminology of ThD as distinct from the PhD. As such, the ThD is usually under the aegis of the divinity or theological school—which you will remember is almost always affiliated with universities—while the PhD is offered under the auspices of the graduate school of arts and sciences at a university.

Although most all seminaries have changed the name from ThD to PhD, certain divinity/theological schools maintain the ThD to distinguish it from a PhD awarded by the graduate (not divinity or theology) school.

For example, that bastion of educational excellence, Harvard, is one of the few American seminaries that retain both the ThD and the PhD. In this context, Harvard Divinity School (www.hds.harvard.edu) offers the ThD while the Faculty of Arts and Sciences (which is not a seminary) awards the PhD. Similarly, Duke University maintains a similar distinction between the divinity school (www.divinity.duke.edu), which offers the ThD for research related exclusively to the church and Christian ministry, and the graduate school at the university, which awards the PhD for purely academic endeavors. In contrast to the prevalent model in the United States, Canada has even more instances of seminaries that offer the ThD.

Possible Sequence for Doctor of Theology in Seminary

Prerequisites	Master of divinity; usually ministerial experience
Language requirements	Passing exams in two to three foreign languages
Coursework	Twelve to fourteen (specialized) courses
Comprehensive examinations	Three to five examinations in areas of discipline(s)
Dissertation	Original research topic of several hundred pages
Total years	Four to six years

Doctor of Philosophy (PhD)

Of all the degrees seminaries offer, the PhD is the highest academically and the most respected. It differs from the degrees discussed directly above in that the PhD is mostly or completely academic, whereas the others may contain more ministerial components as well. The PhD could actually be obtained in most of the areas discussed above; the difference between the two is that the PhD is more research-based. For this reason, the PhD is the appropriate degree sought by those who want to research and write, as well as teach at either the university or the seminary level.

The PhD is the crème de la crème of theological cogitation. Applying for admittance is a consuming process; being admitted into a PhD is even more difficult. The number of applicants for PhDs each decade continues to increase. Being admitted into a PhD program at a seminary—though not quite as difficult as at a university, perhaps—can be extremely challenging. It is best to prepare early and very well.

The PhD is the highest academic degree you can earn. You must choose a specialty before you enter—biblical studies, church history, systematic theology, and so forth—and you must already be quite proficient in that area before you are admitted into the program. What is more, you will need to have a reading proficiency in several languages—both ancient (perhaps Greek, Hebrew, or Latin) and modern (usually German and French or Spanish). After completing the customary two years of coursework, you must take a series of written and oral examinations (comprehensive or preliminary examinations), before writing a lengthy dissertation on an original theme or quandary within theology. Once—or maybe if!—you complete those requirements, you have one more thing to do: defend your dissertation before a few experts in the field.

A ThD is primarily intended for those who will teach at the seminary level, pastor a congregation, or for those who will become leaders in other Christian organizations.

One more thing: as someone who has actually gone through the process of earning a PhD, I can honestly say that you must be very confident of your vocation. A PhD is like a fire that consumes the land. It will take all of your money, time, and energy. If you are married and have children, this degree will affect your family just as much as it will affect you. In this respect, things have changed little historically. In the Middle Ages, for instance, those who actually earned a doctorate in theology were few and far between. The reasons then were the same as today: it took too much time and too much money, and it was the most rigorous of the four major disciplines offered at the medieval university. On the lighter side, however, entering and earning a PhD is a realistic goal. Hundreds of people obtain them each year—but with a cost. I thoroughly enjoyed the process, and I am better for it. But I understand very well that a PhD is not for everyone. Make sure that it is appropriate for your professional objectives. The PhD is necessary for those who intend to pursue one of the following professions:

PhD programs are competitive and rigorous. They will be a challenge to both you and your family.

Professor at a university or seminary

Administrator at a university or seminary

Researcher or writer or other academic

Pastor at a large or intellectual congregation

Possible Sequence for Doctor of Philosophy in Seminary

Prerequisites	Master of divinity or master of arts
Language requirements	Passing exams in two to three foreign languages
Coursework	Twelve to fourteen (specialized) courses
Comprehensive examinations	Three to five examinations in areas of discipline(s)
Dissertation	Original research topic of several hundred pages
Total Years	Four to six years

Ecclesiastical and Civil Degrees
(Only at Certain Roman Catholic Seminaries)

Certain Roman Catholic seminaries make distinctions between two different types or classes of degrees. At some Catholic seminaries—in contrast to Protestant seminaries, for instance—a distinction is sometimes made between those schools that have pontifical charters (signifying that they are directly tied to the Pope in Rome) and those Catholic schools that do not have such charters. Stated another way, certain Catholic seminaries make a distinction between "ecclesiastical" degrees—which train prospective priests and others for specific positions within the Catholic church—and "civil" degrees—which do not necessarily, but may, train prospective priests and others for specific positions within the Catholic church. Whereas regular Catholic seminaries utilize the nomenclature used above when it comes to granting degrees (MDiv, MA, and PhD), seminaries with pontifical charters are entitled to offer *additional* degrees (STB, STL, and STD) in the name of the Holy See in Rome.

Though not exact, the major distinction between civil Catholic degrees and ecclesiastical degrees is the following: civil degrees intentionally prepare students for careers related to research, teaching, and writing in religion and theology—whether within the Catholic church, a different Christian tradition, or a secular institution. Ecclesiastical degrees prepare students for specific careers tied to the Catholic church—whether teaching, research, or leadership. Below are some of the different types of ecclesiastical degrees that certain Catholic seminaries may offer:

- **Bachelor of sacred theology (STB)**—Basic theological degree (roughly equivalent to the master of divinity)
- **Licentiate in sacred theology (STL)**—Advanced theological degree (roughly equivalent to the master of theology)
- **Doctorate of sacred theology (STD)**—Terminal advanced degree (roughly equivalent to doctor of theology)

Summarizing Different Degrees

In the past two chapters, we have covered a good deal of ground when it comes to degrees and programs that seminaries offer. Seminaries have changed considerably over the years concerning the number of programs they offer. Although it is impossible to state with certainty, I would imagine that even more specific and original programs will emerge in the twenty-first century. I particularly foresee more programs being created that have to do with media, technology, counseling, and other underrepresented areas. I also think that more new seminary students will be less interested in pastoral ministry or even Christian ministry—as least as we know it. If I am correct, more programs will have to accommodate these new interests, and I am excited about the possibilities of seeing new programs emerge.

POST-SEMINARY THINGS TO CONSIDER WHILE IN SEMINARY

15

Careers Requiring Ordination or Licensure

For many students, graduating with a seminary degree does not conclude their theological training. Upon graduation they have another aspect of training they must complete. I refer mostly to ordination or certification, which is an additional component to certain students' seminary coursework. The goal of this chapter is to discuss how someone prepares for a profession subsequent to graduation. I will focus on those careers that require some type of certification—whether ordination for pastors or state licensure for counselors and therapists.

Ordination

So you want to be a pastor? Are you sure? Being a pastor is a wonderful vocation, but it is not necessarily a peaceful or relaxing profession. Those who want to become pastors and priests will undergo extensive evaluation by their individual congregations, their denominations, themselves, and even, perhaps, their seminaries. Your life—and that of your spouse and children as well, if you are married or have a family—will be forever "public." In order to succeed as a minister, then, and in order to validate yourself as one who is equipped for this profession, there are certain steps that your denomination or particular tradition will require you to take. In fact, ordination is not actually administered by a seminary. Seminaries cannot ordain anybody. For this reason, it does not matter whether you go to a denominational or nondenominational school. The particular denomination or church body ordains a candidate once he or she has fulfilled all of the many requirements that are set by the denomination.

The specific procedure for ordination varies according to denomination or religious tradition, that is to say, whether you are Catholic, Orthodox, Protestant, or Episcopalian. Some denominations are quite rigorous and require prospective clergy to undergo a process of ordination lasting a number of years. Others—particularly Protestant nondenominational churches—are less rigorous in their ordination procedure. Although they certainly do not just ordain anyone who wants to become a pastor, they are less demanding than other more historic theological traditions.

Six Steps toward Ordination

Unfortunately, it is impossible to say with certainty how the process of ordination will be carried out in your denomination or tradition of faith. Every denomination administers this process differently, in one way or another. Even within Protestant traditions, there are myriad ways that denominations proceed when ordaining candidates. Because this is the case, the six steps to ordination that we will discuss below are very general; these are six broad steps—framed in my own words—that many denominations will utilize in the process of ordaining a potential candidate. The specific process of ordination in your tradition may differ; be sure to consult your denomination for more exact information on ordination.

The specific procedure for ordination varies according to denomination or religious tradition.

COMMUNAL AND INDIVIDUAL CALLING (SENSE OF VOCATION)

The first step toward ordination is receiving and acknowledging a specific "calling" to pastoral or priestly ministry. In technical terms, this refers to "vocation," a word that comes from the Latin word meaning "to call." Many contend that pastoral ministry is a vocation and not a profession. By this they mean that pastoring and ministering are not just what one *does* (professionally), but what one *is* (vocationally). To have a profession simply means that one knows certain things that others do not; to have a vocation means that one *is* something that others are not, that is, one who serves God through the edification and upbuilding of God's people.

In this respect, when speaking of "calling" it is not too long before one detects that the subject—the one who calls—becomes just as important as the object, namely, you! The subject of this calling we believe to be the Spirit of God. It is God who calls individuals to the ministry. Nevertheless, Christians throughout the centuries have discerned a pattern: God normally calls people to the ministry through *other* people. We in the Western part of the world often ignore the role that others play in our calling; instead, we tend to validate our calling from God individualistically, and only afterward do we seek confirmation from pastors or friends.

> 66 What pastors do is a function of who pastors are. 99
>
> *William Willimon*
> *(author and bishop)*

Whatever the exact process of receiving our calling, however, the lesson to be learned is as follows: There needs to be both a subject (the one who calls) and an object (the one called) when it comes to pastoral ministry. We know who the object is: you. The question now becomes, Who is the subject? Who has called you into the ministry? We hope that it is God who has called you—by means of the church. The church—that community of faith composed of changed but imperfect human beings—is the vehicle God typically utilizes when calling someone into the ministry. It need not matter whether you were the first person to identify this call or whether it was the church; what is important is that there is an internal and an external calling. The reason why an external call is necessary is obvious: the ministry, as the word originally meant in Greek, refers to "service." Those who minister are those who serve. And it is the church you serve as an ordained minister.

SEMINARY EDUCATION (MASTER OF DIVINITY)

After someone has been called into the ministry, what usually follows is the need for specialized theological education, that is, seminary. Most denominations require that potential ministerial candidates graduate from seminary. The degree they prefer, as was discussed in the previous two chapters, is called the master of divinity. This degree expressly prepares students for pastoral ministry. It will equip you for the vocation of pastor, and it is usually the major step that prospective ministers will have to take in their progress toward ordained ministry.

DENOMINATIONAL ASSOCIATION AND ASSISTANCE

The third step involved in the process of ordained ministry is initiating and maintaining a relationship with your denomination or church body. This step, however, does not occur only after graduating from seminary. Rather, it usually occurs before, during, and after seminary. After the first step of being called to the ministry, in other words,

Most denominations prefer that prospective ministers earn the master of divinity.

the second and third steps overlap. You should be in communication with your denomination or local church as soon as you are in a position to attend seminary—and preferably even before that. (The terminologies for the leaders of specific denominations vary from tradition to tradition: diocese, presbytery, synod, and so forth.) Your regional denominational leaders will then presumably place you "under care," as some traditions put it, as an intern or candidate for the remainder of your time in seminary. You will meet periodically with the leaders of your denomination and apprise them of your progress in seminary. This may be formal or informal, but your denomination will want to be in close contact with you through this process in one way or another.

The internship is time for you to gain invaluable experience and to learn if you are really able and still want to be a minister.

REQUIRED INTERNSHIP OR MENTORED MINISTRY

The fourth step toward ordination involves working with a local church or other related organization within your specific denomination. This is usually referred to as an internship. The length varies from tradition to tradition. Some require at least a year-long internship, which occurs either simultaneously with or after your seminary education. During an internship the candidate is scrutinized by both congregation and denomination to ensure that he or she is suitable for ordained ministry. It is a trial run as well as a time of learning and growth. However, it is not a trial run for the congregation or denomination alone; your time of internship is also designed to confirm whether *you* believe that you are called to ordained ministry. While you are interning, you will have the opportunity to test your giftedness for the ministry, to apply what you have learned in seminary, and to decide whether the ordained life is what you had envisioned. The internship is an extremely important component of your development as a minister.

EXAMINATIONS

The fifth step that you may take in the process of ordination after graduating from seminary and completing your required field experience or internship is that of denominational examinations. By this point you will have learned the denomination's history and understood, affirmed, and articulated its core beliefs; and you will have internalized its essential doctrines. Frequently, your denominational committee will administer oral and even written exams to certify fully that you will represent the denomination faithfully. Your denomination will take this process very seriously, as it is the last phase of your training before you are an official and certified representative of the denomination.

ORDINATION

The final step toward pastoral ministry is the actual ordination. This is a solemn occasion—the culmination of the intense process that you will have endured for the sake of serving God's people as a minister. Usually the ceremony is small, with only your family and closest friends present, in addition to important denominational figures. Many ceremonies also include an important individual in your denomination, who will preach to you a sermon and present you with a challenge to remain faithful to the gospel as God's ambassador to the church. At the conclusion there may be a laying-on of hands—a very ancient Christian tradition—by your denominational leaders, which officially represents God's anointing on your ministry. There will also be prayer and other admonitions. This ceremony is a significant component to your ministry, and it is designed to serve as a real and visible manifestation of your calling to the ordained life when you may perhaps be led to doubt this calling at any point in your ministry in the future. If you pursue ordained ministry, your ordination will positively reinforce your calling throughout your career.

> 66 The Bishop's charge to the candidates on the eve of ordination was always most impressive, "Tomorrow I shall say to you, 'wilt thou, wilt thou, wilt thou?' But there will come a day when Another will say, 'hast thou, hast thou, hast thou?'" 99
>
> *Charles Gore*
> *(Anglican bishop and author)*

Summary of Steps to Follow toward Ordination

1. Discuss with the local church your desire to enter ordained ministry.
2. Locate and attend a seminary (usually enrolling in the master of divinity).
3. In your new area (if you moved), find a church affiliated with your tradition.
4. Meet periodically with your denominational leaders and local church.
5. You will then undergo an examination process. This will require you to fill out a good deal of paperwork regarding your theological views, background, financial situation, and many other questions. You may have oral and written tests as well.
6. The ordination is the culminating process after graduation and an internship.

A Specific Look at the Ordination Process

Perhaps it would be appropriate to end our discussion about the process of ordination by providing a real example from a specific denomination. Every denomination ordains its clergypersons in a slightly differ-ent way. For this reason, I have chosen one denomination as a tangible example of the ordination process in general. The denomination that I have selected is the Presbyterian Church (USA), a mainline denomination in North America. I have chosen this denomination because its website (www. pcusa.org) is very informative and user-friendly for those who are contemplating seminary and ordination. If you are thinking about a career in pastoral ministry—regardless of your theological affiliation—I think you would benefit from this website. Below I have rephrased some of the steps to-ward ordination into my own words. These are very general steps that I am discussing, to offer you a rough guide of the ordination process. Once again, be sure to consult your denomination of choice for more specific information.

To help us see how a specific denomination conducts the ordination process, I have chosen the Presbyterian Church (USA), which provides a wonderful website about this process at www.pcsusa.org.

Process of Contemplating the Ministry in the Presbyterian Church (USA)

1. Internal Call to Ministry—The prospective minister experiences an inner call to the vocation of pastoral ministry.
2. External Call to Ministry—The Christian community affirms the internal call of the prospective minister.
3. Specific Call to Ministry—A specific congregation requests the min-ister to pastor its congregation.

Ordination Process in the Presbyterian Church (USA)

1. The prospective minister expresses his or her desire to enter the pastoral ministry to the local governing board of the denomination. (This can be done only after a person has been an active member of the church for a minimum of six months.)
2. If the governing board approves, the prospective minister is evaluated and explores the possibility of being a pastor for the next couple of years.
3. The prospective minister then becomes an official candidate—given that the governing board and the candidate are content with the pas-toral process.

4. The prospective minister will have finished a college degree and will need to complete a seminary degree (usually the master of divinity).
5. Afterward, the candidate must pass national exams set by the denomination—which covers such areas as biblical studies, church history, theology, Presbyterian doctrine, and worship.
6. Once the candidate passes the exams, he or she must undergo one final approval by the denomination (with regard to pastoral fitness, moral rectitude, and spiritual maturity).
7. The candidate is officially ordained and will then be called to a particular congregation to serve as an ordained minister.

What Ordination Means

Now that we have isolated the specific process of ordination, it is important that we briefly discuss the actual significance of ordination. I begin by stating the obvious: ordination is not for everyone. Becoming ordained is not simply what one does because he or she has graduated from seminary. It is a process that you undertake only after being called into the ministry and having this calling confirmed by your congregation, your seminary, and those you will serve. Ordination means that you have been officially approved by a particular denomination or local church for professional ministry. It means that you are qualified to preach, administer the sacraments, admonish congregants, officiate at weddings and funerals, and lead at many other functions. You will be expected to lead a respectable life and will be looked upon as a leader in your community.

Becoming ordained is not simply what one does because he or she has graduated from seminary. It is a process that you undertake only after being called into the ministry.

Ordination and the Law

Being ordained, however, is not just a religious designation. It entails a specific status in the eyes of the federal government, particularly the Internal Revenue Service in the United States. Ordained ministers maintain a certain tax status as a result of their ordination. It is one of the wonderful benefits, some might say, of the clergy. According to the law in the United States, ordained ministers are eligible for a housing allowance. Clergypersons are allowed to exclude expenses from their gross annual income that were spent on items for their primary house of residence. Thus, a purchase, for instance, of a couch or table could qualify for this exemption. In addition

Generally speaking, counselor and therapist (and even psychotherapist) are interchangeable professional titles.

to this housing allowance there is one more important component to ordination with respect to the law. As an ordained minister, you are certified by your state to unite couples in holy matrimony.

Certification/Licensure

Besides ordination for pastoral ministry, certification from the state is required for other professions chosen by seminary graduates. I am particularly referring to those seminarians who will seek state licensure as a counselor or therapist. (Students who enter programs in education at seminary, by the way, typically do not pursue licensure.) If you enter seminary in pursuit of licensure as a counselor or therapist, you will have many components to your education that will supplement your coursework. There will be supervised field hours, state requirements, and several other components. This is because counseling is a profession that requires a great deal of time and preparation.

Four Steps to Follow toward Licensure as a Counselor or Therapist

In this section I discuss some of the steps that you will need to take in order to become licensed as a counselor or therapist. As I do so, you must bear in mind that the process of licensure varies from state to state, specialty to specialty, and school to school. In fact, depending on your professional objectives, licensure may not even be required or advantageous. For those of you who are in need of state licensure, we will discuss the steps that you will most likely need to take in order to meet the requirements of your state. It is important that you contact the state board in your area for the specific guidelines and regulations for the license you seek—in addition to the requirements at your seminary of choice. The following steps are thus only approximate; they are designed to help you think in general terms about what needs to be done if you are in need of licensure.

Key Terms Related to Counseling

Christian counseling	Counseling from an explicitly Christian point of view
Clinical psychology	Assesses and treats psychological problems
Counseling psychology	Addresses minor and normal problems
Psychology	Scientific study of human behavior and the mind
Social work	Focuses on the social context of individuals' problems
Marriage and family therapy	Specializes in family and marriage-related problems

DETERMINING WHETHER YOUR PROFESSIONAL OBJECTIVES REQUIRE LICENSURE

The first step to take when considering a profession in counseling or therapy is determining whether you need state licensure. This depends completely upon your professional objectives. There are essentially two options available: (1) if you intend to work for a non-Christian organization, you will probably need to obtain licensure; (2) if you intend to work for a Christian organization, you may or may not need to obtain state licensure. The need to obtain licensure depends upon each person and each specific position, and upon his or her professional objectives upon graduating from seminary. You should speak with your church, your seminary of choice, your seminary faculty adviser, and perhaps your state to determine whether certification is necessary.

ENROLLING IN A SPECIFIC PROGRAM (MASTER OF ARTS)

The second step to take after deciding whether to seek certification is that of locating a specific program. Especially if you are pursuing state licensure, remember that not all seminaries collaborate with the state toward licensure. Because seminaries traditionally prepared students for ordination and other careers related specifically to the church—and because counseling degrees offered at seminary are a fairly recent phenomenon—they are perhaps lagging behind the typical Christian university that would offer a graduate degree in counseling.

Possible State Licensure for Seminary Graduates

Licensed Marriage and Family Therapist (LMFT)

Licensed Professional Counselor (LPC)

Licensed Clinical Professional Counselor (LCPC)

There are, however, many seminaries these days that offer distinguished programs related to counseling—including those that prepare students for state licensure. Usually the program that correlates with these students' objectives is the master of arts in the area they choose to minister: marriage and family therapy, clinical psychology (which may require further study), and so forth. The typical seminary degree, the master of divinity, is usually *not* a degree that leads to state licensure in counseling—unless perhaps it is a joint master of divinity degree, but that is still not too common. If you are pursuing ordination or pastoral ministry in conjunction with counseling or therapy, you should probably enroll in a joint master of divinity

If you are interested in licensure as a counselor or therapist, consult the following: American Counselors Association (www.counselor.org), American Psychological Association (www.apa.org), and the National Board for Certified Counselors (www.nbcc.org).

program. Otherwise you should simply enroll in a master of arts degree in your particular area. For some, an eventual doctorate may even be necessary.

There is a plethora of master's degrees in seminary that are related in some way to counseling. Some are general, others are specific; some are designed exclusively for state licensure; and some prepare students for enrolling in doctorates. If you are interested in licensure, many excellent programs at seminaries across North America are available. Ashland Theological Seminary (www.ashland.edu/seminary) in Ohio, for instance, has a Master of Arts in Clinical Pastoral Counseling; Biblical Theological Seminary (www.biblical.edu), outside of Philadelphia, offers a Master of Arts in Counseling; Providence Theological Seminary (http://prov.ca), in Manitoba, offers a Master of Arts in Counseling Psychology; while Trinity Evangelical Divinity School (www.tiu.edu/divinity), outside of Chicago, offers both a Master of Arts in Counseling Ministries—for those not pursuing state licensure—and a Master of Arts in Counseling Psychology, for those who are.

Sample of Counseling Degrees at Seminary

MA in Biblical Counseling

MA in Christian Counseling

MA in Counseling

MA in Counseling Psychology

MA in Marriage and Family Counseling

MA in Marriage and Family Therapy

MA in Pastoral Counseling

Dual Master of Divinity + Master of Arts

What's more, Reformed Theological Seminary (www.rts.edu) in Jackson, Mississippi, has a Master of Arts in Marriage and Family Counseling; Louisville Presbyterian Theological Seminary (www.lpts.edu) offers a Master of Arts in Marriage and Family Therapy; and Fuller Theological Seminary (www.fuller.edu) in southern California maintains a complete school of psychology for interested candidates, offering both master's and doctoral degrees related to counseling and psychology.

Satisfying Course Requirements and Internship

The third step in the process toward licensure is graduating from seminary with the appropriate degree and satisfying all degree and state requirements. This process is twofold. First, the requirements for a degree that leads to licensure are detailed and specific. You must meet all of the requirements: passing courses, completing internships, and so forth. The second aspect of the process relates to the state. The state sets many requirements for licensure, such as the following: graduating with the appropriate degree and even a set of courses not required for the program; interning and completing a specific number of hours of supervised fieldwork; completing supervised postgraduate counseling hours that vary widely from state to state; filling out appropriate paperwork; and undergoing a criminal check and perhaps even a mental-health examination. Once again, be sure to contact your local state or institution for the specific requirements and internships.

Applying for and Passing a State Examination

The fourth and last step toward obtaining licensure is applying for and ultimately passing state examinations in your specialty. By now you will have met all of the above requirements, which will have taken several years. The culmination of this process is passing the state examinations. These tests are specifically designed to evaluate the knowledge that you have gained in the classroom and through your clinical or supervised work.

Depending on what area of counseling or therapy you specialize in during seminary, you will pursue licensure in that specific field. For instance, if you earn a Master of Arts in Marriage and Family Therapy from seminary, you will probably attempt certification as a licensed marriage and family therapist (LMFT). Or if you enroll in a Master of Arts in Counseling from seminary, you will most likely pursue certification as a licensed professional counselor (LPC). Conversely, if you want to become a clinical psychologist, you will likely need to earn a doctorate in addition to a master's degree from seminary—either a PhD or a PsyD in clinical psychology (see the fourteenth chapter for information on advanced seminary degrees). Although Fuller Theological Seminary (www.fuller.edu) offers both these degrees, they are not traditionally offered at seminary.

Just as you do not automatically become a lawyer upon graduating from law school, so too you do not necessarily become a counselor upon graduating from seminary. If you are pursuing licensure, you will have to pass state examinations after graduation.

Summary of Steps to Follow toward Licensure

1. Decide whether you intend to be licensed (by the state).
2. Learn the state requirements where you are likely to work after graduation.
3. Locate a seminary that offers a degree that specifically prepares students for state licensure (usually the master of arts, *not* a master of divinity).
4. Complete the degree, all field experience and supervised hours, and satisfy all state requirements.
5. Apply for and pass the state examinations.
6. Get off the couch, do not forget to network, and get a job!

If you earn a Master of Arts in Marriage and Family Therapy from seminary, you will probably pursue licensure as a marriage and family therapist (LFMT). Or if you earn a Master of Arts in Counseling, you will probably pursue licensure as a licensed professional counselor (LPC).

Certification as a Teacher

Students interested in teacher certification should pursue a master's degree from a Christian university rather than a seminary. This is not because seminaries are necessarily opposed to cooperating with the state toward licensure. Instead, it has to do with the purpose of seminary in contrast to the focus of a university. Seminaries typically prepare students for Christian ministry, whereas Christian universities prepare students for both Christian and non-Christian professions. Generally speaking, I would recommend the following: those teachers with interest in state licensure should most likely enroll in a master's degree at a Christian university, while those who want to teach in a Christian setting such as a church or secondary Christian school—institutions that do not ordinarily require certification—could attend seminary.

Those interested in teacher certification should pursue a master's degree in education from a Christian university rather than a seminary.

Entering a Profession

For some of you, discussions about attending and graduating from seminary as well as entering a profession that takes years to prepare for may seem like an eternity away. This is understandable, but you may be surprised at how quickly schooling comes and goes. The key is to be prepared and to know what to expect. In this chapter you learned how to prepare for ordination and licensure, and we discussed the process that you will need to take to meet the requirements set by seminary and the state. The next chapter also discusses entering a profession but focuses specifically on those careers that do not require ordination or licensure.

16

Careers Not Requiring Certification

When I entered seminary, I was not certain what I would do after graduation. Initially, I had thought about missions. Before too long, however, I turned my attention to academics and a possible career as a university or seminary professor. By the time I graduated from seminary the second time—with the master of divinity—I had taken a job as a high school Spanish teacher. Since then, I have been writing a book about seminary! Who knows what the future holds for me, but I hope your time in seminary results in a specific profession that is ideal for your gifts, abilities, and interests. In this chapter we will observe some common professions that seminary students enter upon graduation. In contrast to the professions we looked at in the last chapter, this chapter focuses on those careers not requiring certification.

Missions, Church Planting, or Evangelism (Discipleship)

Seminary has always been the place to go for those interested in missions, church planting, and evangelism. Although the nature of missions has changed dramatically since the creation of the first seminaries in North America a couple of hundred years ago, seminaries graduate many students each year who will pursue careers related to missions, church planting, and

Missions, church planting, and evangelism are professions that often overlap. Traditionally, missions and church planting (creating new indigenous churches) were done overseas, while evangelism and discipleship (mentoring Christians) were not. Today, each of these professions can be done either internationally or domestically.

evangelism. There are important differences among these careers, but they all relate in similar ways, and there is a good deal of overlap. And contrary to what may have been the case a hundred years ago, for instance, missionaries, church planters, and evangelists live and work in North America as well as in other parts of the world.

A sense of calling, fitness, and ability are all important if you choose to be a missionary, a church planter, or an evangelist. After you and your community of faith have determined that you have the right temperament and personality for these professions, you will then need to learn more about specifics. If you want to enter a career in missions or church planting, for instance, the process will probably be very similar. Often these two careers require their workers to raise their own financial support. Probably two of the most common ways of gaining this support are by partnering with a specific missionary organization or with a specific denomination or a group of churches. These bodies will assist you through what will probably be a very lengthy process—in the case of fundraising, that is. The best place to begin is your local church, denominational headquarters, or another missionary organization.

Possible Employers in Missions, Church Planting, Evangelism, and Discipleship

Local church
Denominational headquarters
Missionary organization
Parachurch organization
School (secondary, college, seminary)
Secular employer

Careers in evangelism, by contrast, may or may not require you to raise your own financial support. Some churches or parachurches (Christian organizations that work alongside the church) actually employ evangelists. In fact, evangelists in some churches are simply alternative names for pastors or preachers. In this case, the discussion about pastoral ministry in the previous chapter would directly apply to this career.

If you intend to enter a career related to missions, church planting, evangelism, or discipleship on a full-time basis, you will probably need to enter seminary and enroll in one of two degrees. The standard seminary degree, the master of divinity, is always an appropriate and suitable degree for any full-time Christian ministry. However, it is not the only—or even the best—degree for those interested in one of these different careers.

Many seminaries these days offer excellent programs related to the master of arts degree that prepare students for these professions. Church of God Theological Seminary (www.cogts.edu) in Cleveland, for instance, provides a Master of Arts in Discipleship and Christian Formation for those interested in mentoring and discipleship. Mennonite Brethren Biblical Seminary (www.mbseminary.edu), in Fresno, California, offers a Master of Arts in Intercultural Mission. Moreover, Southeastern Baptist Theological Seminary (www.sebts.edu), in Wake Forest, South Carolina, offers a Master of Divinity with concentrations in either North American Church Planting or International Church Planting that directly prepares students for careers related to starting and maintaining new churches.

Steps toward Entering Missions, Church Planting, or Evangelism (Discipleship)

1. Have a sense of calling confirmed by your local church, denomination, or other specific Christian institution or agency.
2. Enroll in a degree program at seminary (master of arts or master of divinity with concentration in one of the above fields).
3. Speak with your local church, denomination, missionary organization, or other parachurch body about career possibilities and financial support.
4. Graduate from seminary and fulfill any fieldwork or mandatory experience.

Teaching and Research (Academia)

Every year several students enter their respective seminaries of choice with the intention of one day becoming academics. If you want to become a professor at either a seminary or a Christian university—even possibly at a secular university—you will need to obtain additional training and experience after earning your first theological degree from seminary. As I stated in the previous chapters on seminary degrees, the master of divinity is the classic seminary degree that will usually encompass every student's professional objectives—though not everyone's, of course.

If you are intent on entering a career related to teaching and research, you can pursue either the master of divinity or the master of arts. Either one is usually acceptable; a good rule of thumb is to earn the master of divinity if you want to teach at a seminary, but a master of arts (in whatever discipline you will study—whether biblical studies, spirituality, or so forth) if you are planning on a career at a Christian (or secular) university. (Also remember that those who intend to teach at the secondary level—whether at a private or a public school—should enroll in a master's degree in education at a Christian university rather than a seminary.)

Although teaching at the seminary or university level is a wonderful profession, be prepared to undergo a dozen years of training, intense competition, and less-than-huge paychecks!

After earning the first seminary degree, students who want to teach at the college or seminary level will eventually need to obtain a doctorate. What type of doctoral program you enroll in depends on your specific objectives and what you hope to teach. If you want to become a counseling professor, for instance, you should probably pursue state licensure sometime after graduating from seminary with a first seminary degree, that is, a master's degree in a related field. After gaining some practical experience, you will then usually enroll in either a PhD or a PsyD (doctor of psychology) at a Christian or a non-Christian university.

Or perhaps you want to become a professor of preaching (homiletics) at a seminary one day. Initially, you will need to earn a master of divinity degree (as opposed to a master of arts) at seminary. Afterward, you will probably seek employment as a pastor at a church for a few years to gain some ministry and preaching experience. Your last step is to locate a seminary (and not necessarily a university, though that is possible) that offers a doctor of ministry with a specialization in preaching, or a ThD or PhD in an area related to homiletics or preaching.

If you want to teach at the seminary or university level, you will need at least two postbaccalaureate degrees: a master's degree and a terminal degree in your discipline—almost always a doctorate.

If you want to teach one of the more traditionally academic theological subjects—biblical studies, systematic theology, or church history—you have two general options. The first is to enroll in a ThD or PhD at a seminary after earning the MA or MDiv. (The DMin does not generally prepare students to teach academic subjects.) The second is to enroll in a PhD at a Christian or secular university. However, whatever field of theology you intend to teach in—regardless of whether you want to do so at a seminary or a university—it is important to speak with your adviser at seminary for more specific details about a career relating to teaching and research.

Steps toward Becoming a Professor (Seminary or University)

1. Have a sense of calling for academics, teaching, and research.
2. Earn a basic degree such as a master of arts or master of divinity in your area of interest.
3. Get some experience (teaching or otherwise) if at all possible.
4. Enroll in a doctoral program in your area of interest. This will probably include taking the GRE (Graduate Record Examination) or the MAT (Miller Analogies Test), as well as passing written examinations in a couple of foreign languages.
5. Expect to spend a lot of money and a lot of time along the way!

Worship, Music, or Liturgy

The last decades have witnessed an increase in the number of seminary programs related to worship, liturgy, and music ministries. As you might expect, music ministries go by many different names in the Christian world, and each tradition makes use of its own musical instruments and preferences. Some more historic traditions, for instance, lean toward the organ or piano, while other churches prefer more contemporary music styles. Many churches and denominations have struggled with the question of different styles of worship, and each seminary and tradition offers its own unique way of worshiping God through the medium of music.

There are more opportunities today than ever before for those interested in music-related ministries. However, you will learn that there are only a few programs that you would want to attend. If your idea of music ministry, for instance, is playing the organ in a church setting, you will most likely not want to attend a seminary that is part of a tradition that uses only electric guitars in worship services! Similarly, if you happen to be a Pentecostal who wants to lead worship every Sunday, you will probably not enroll in a music program at a Catholic seminary. My advice, therefore, for those pursuing music and worship ministries is to find a seminary that is very closely affiliated with one's own church tradition and preference.

Possible Names for Seminary Programs Related to Music

Master of Arts in Church Music

Master of Arts in Worship

Master of Music

Master of Sacred Music

Master of Liturgy

The most appropriate degree for those with interests in worship would be any type of master's degree from seminary related to liturgy, music, or worship *other* than the master of divinity. These programs go by a variety of names; accordingly, it is difficult to say which is the best degree for your circumstances. The Interdenominational Theological Center (www.itc.edu) in Atlanta, for instance, offers a Master of Arts in Church Music; New Orleans Baptist Theological Seminary (www.nobts.edu) offers a Master of Music in Church Music; the Department of Theology at the University of Notre Dame (http://theology.nd.edu) in Indiana offers a Master of Sacred Music; Mundelein Seminary at the University of St. Mary of the Lake (www.usml.edu) outside of Chicago offers a Master of Arts in Liturgy; and Calvin Theological Seminary (www.calvinseminary.edu) in Grand Rapids, Michigan, offers a Master of Arts in Worship. Although each of these programs relates to music and worship ministries, they all differ when it comes to styles and preference of worship.

Steps toward Entering a Career in Church Music and Worship

1. Have a sense of calling confirmed by your local church or religious tradition.
2. Enroll in a master's degree related to music (usually not the master of divinity).
3. Get experience with a local church or other institution while in seminary.
4. Eventually obtain a job in a local church, work independently, or become a teacher (at the primary or secondary school level; for college or seminary teaching, you will most likely need to earn a doctorate in music).
5. Write and perform your own music and become a celebrity!

Education, Administration, and Leadership

The last specific professions that we will look at in this chapter that do not require certification are careers related to education, administration, and even leadership. More and more seminaries these days are catering to this form of ministry, and you might be surprised at exactly how many programs are available for those interested in teaching or leadership positions. Those who enroll in programs in education usually intend to teach at the primary or secondary level at a Christian institution or at a local church large enough to sustain a full-time, or even a part-time, educator. Because churches and many Christian primary and secondary schools do not expect their teachers to be certified by the state, entering a program in education at seminary is ideal for those seeking such positions.

The prospects for those with a degree in leadership (or administration) are really quite varied. It depends on the person, his or her background and goals, and the program attended.

Those who enroll in programs related to leadership or administration have varied objectives upon graduation: Some desire to work at churches or denominations in specific kinds of leadership capacities (particularly at larger churches); some will work in parachurches or other Christian organizations in the roles of leadership or administration; others will find jobs as principals or administrators at Christian schools; while still others will pursue careers in leadership in the secular workplace. In this respect, the prospects for those with such a degree are really quite varied. It depends on the person, his or her background and goals, and the specific program attended.

There are dozens of seminaries that offer excellent programs other than the master of divinity related to Christian education. For instance, Covenant Theological Seminary (www.covenantseminary.edu) in St. Louis offers a Master of Arts in Educational Ministries; Campbell University Divinity School (www.campbell.edu/divinity) in North Carolina offers a Master of Arts in Christian Education; Newman Theological College (www.newman.edu) in Alberta, Canada, offers a Master of Religious Education; and Union Theological Seminary and Presbyterian School of Christian Education (www.union-psce.edu) in Richmond, Virginia, offers a Master of Arts in Christian Education as well as a PhD. The following are examples of seminaries that offer programs related to leadership and administration: Asbury Theological Seminary (www.asburyseminary.edu) in Kentucky offers a Master of Arts in Christian Leadership; Golden Gate Baptist Theological Seminary (www.ggbts.edu) in California has a Master of Arts in Educational Leadership; and Phoenix Seminary (www.phoenixseminary.edu) offers a Master of Arts in Biblical Leadership.

Other Career Options

Seminarians are no longer interested exclusively in pastoral ministry or related careers. For those of you in this situation—particularly if none of the professions in the previous or present chapter have addressed adequately what you want to pursue upon graduation—I would like to discuss with you what to think about and do while in seminary so that you can graduate with a specific professional objective in mind. This section is especially designed for those who either are about to enter seminary or are still in their initial years at seminary.

While in seminary, always be asking yourself this question: What has God called me to do with this seminary training?

As the old expression goes, "the sky is the limit" when it comes to seminary education these days. The trend is for education in general—which of course includes seminary education—to become more and more specialized, often with a cross-fertilization of various subjects or disciplines. This trend will no doubt create many new professions in the future, and it is an exciting time to attend seminary. However, this trend may or may not apply to your specific profession. Whether it does or doesn't, however, the following steps will, hopefully, enable you to think more clearly about what it is that you are called to do as well as how you can prepare along the way to do it.

Four Steps to Follow toward Discerning a Career from Seminary

Although it may not seem so now, seminary will go by very quickly. Before you know it, you will be graduating. In an ideal world you would know exactly what you want to do upon graduation. However, in our not-so-ideal world it may take months or even years to discern what you are best suited for after graduation. For this reason you need to be constantly thinking of the future and what profession you are called to. Remember that seminary is a professional school, which means that it is training you for a profession of some kind. Therefore, be mindful of how you might be able to apply what you are learning to a career objective—whatever that might be. There are several ways to do this: by talking with professors, friends, and your local church; by concentrating on a particular subject that you enjoy; or by learning what you are gifted in through service in the church or a specific community. In this section we will discuss these steps in detail.

Networking

Like other graduate programs at universities, seminary involves networking or connection making. By *networking* I mean interacting with other students and staff and being in dialogue with them about your interests and objectives. It means getting to know your classmates and professors, attending school functions, and staying involved with the happenings of your school. Networking can prove extremely helpful years after graduation when you are in need of a job or a referral. This is especially the case if you attend a seminary from a particular denominational or theological heritage. Networking can generate a circle of contacts that can be mutually beneficial.

By networking, however, I do not mean manipulation or taking advantage of people. I know of many graduate programs at other universities where networking involves flattery and deception. Christian networking should be based on truth and honesty; it is about making and maintaining healthy and mutually salutary relationships. Networking—more than anything perhaps—has to do with being social and getting to know people. It is the natural consequence of camaraderie and friendship among colleagues and associates.

Seminary goes by very quickly. For this reason, always be preparing for your future goals.

Networking is about being involved in a community and being vulnerable and open about your circumstances and needs.

Prayer and Discussion

A second step that I would like to speak about is prayer and discussion. Perhaps you remember the verse in the book of James that states "the prayer of a righteous man is powerful and effective" (James 5:16 NIV). Prayer is one of the most simple yet most profound things that we can do as Christians. It is at the heart of the Christian life, and I can think of few more important places to begin when considering what our vocations should be. This is especially the case for those who intend to enroll in seminary. As Jesus once said, "Ask and it will be given to you" (Matt. 7:7 NIV). Based on this statement, have you asked God to reveal to you what your profession should be upon graduation? Have you even asked God to reveal to you whether you should attend seminary? I trust that you have. If you have, persist in your prayers; if you have not, I would encourage you to begin asking.

There is another very important component that is related to prayer when considering a career upon graduation. That is discussion with mentors, friends, and families. When it comes down to it, probably nobody knows you better than your friends and family. As a result, it only makes sense that you would discuss with them your plans during and after seminary. They, of all people, will be aware of certain traits or characteristics that will enable you to excel (or not excel!) in any particular profession. In a related way, your minister or mentor should also be able to offer you keen insight about your gifts and shortcomings. I believe that these two—prayer and discussion—are like the chicken and the egg. It is not important whether you will be first directed to the right profession through prayer or discussion. It is important only that these components work together in determining what you need to pursue as a career.

Because your friends and family know you the best, seek them out for counsel about what you should do for a profession.

IDENTIFYING COURSES/SUBJECTS OF INTEREST

I remember it clearly. It was my first class of seminary—an introductory course in New Testament Greek. Even before the class had ended that day, I was certain of one thing: I was going to teach Greek one day! I have heard other seminarians say similar things. Perhaps when you are in seminary, you will discover a class that you absolutely love. If this is the case, I would recommend that you pursue this subject matter further.

Let us say, for instance, that you discover a great interest in counseling while in seminary. During your first course in counseling, you find that you enjoy not just learning how to interact with people but even theories of counseling and specific techniques. This interest of yours in counseling may be a signal that you are just right for a career in counseling—but, then again, it could be a phase or simply one interest among many. What you have to do next is evaluate this interest.

During your next semester take yet another course in counseling. This time make an appointment with the professor, and discuss with her or him your interest in counseling, asking questions about possible career prospects. Determine whether you have the right temperament and abilities to counsel effectively: Are you a good listener? Do you have a habit of interrupting people when they talk? Do you enjoy helping people? Pursue this interest until it is either readily evident that you were made to be a counselor or until your interest wanes and you discover a greater subject of interest.

Finding your Giftedness through Experience

The last step that we will discuss when deciding upon a career—discerning your giftedness—is related to the previous step on discovering an area of interest. This is because there is a great likelihood that you will excel in that what you enjoy. As I have noted above, I would like to encourage you to work part time or perhaps intern with a particular organization related to your area of interest before or during seminary. I do not recommend this just for the sake of gaining important experience—as helpful as that will certainly be; instead, think of this time as a way to discern your giftedness in ministry. Although people may not communicate to you what they believe you do poorly, people will often convey to you what they think you do well. When they do so, pay special attention to their comments. Perhaps you may discover a pattern to people's comments, and this pattern may direct you to an area of the ministry that you can pursue as a career.

If you follow this advice, you may be surprised at what you find. It is not infrequently the case that other people are able to better identify what we do well than we ourselves are able to identify. This actually makes complete sense, for Christian ministry is not about ourselves; it is about serving others—about serving God's people by means of specific gifts that God has given us. By simply taking the time to work a few hours a week or even a month at a particular organization related to Christian ministry, it is my hope that you will discern—through direct feedback or indirect comments—a talent that God has given you for the edification of the community of faith.

One of the best things that you can do both before and during seminary is to get experience in whatever form of ministry you are interested in.

Summarizing Career Opportunities

In this chapter we have talked about how one goes from seminarian to professional. This process involves much more than simply taking courses and passing them. Instead it involves finding the right program, working diligently, networking, interning and getting experience, introspection, prayer, and providence. We have additionally discussed what steps you should take if you are still in the process of discovering what aspect of the ministry you are called to pursue. For some, this process may take longer than for others; if so, do not be discouraged. Rather, be persistent in prayer and discussion, and continue to pursue areas of interest. I am hopeful that before long God and your community of faith will direct you to the vocation that you were designed for. Until then, however, the fast-food industry is always in need of starving seminarians!

In all seriousness, I pray that you will discover the vocation that is perfect for you in every way. In contrast to seminarians a hundred years ago, many students are pursuing careers not related directly to the church. And many of those who are pursuing church- or ministry-related careers are doing so in a way that is perhaps very different from those a couple of generations ago. Whatever path you are directed to follow, I hope that you will look back upon your seminary education as a positive component to both your personal and professional development. I hope that you will apply what you have learned in seminary both to your life and to your vocation with all integrity, humility, creativity, devotion, and concern for those around you.

Always listen to compliments others give you: It may be God's way of communicating where your giftedness lies.

GENERAL THINGS TO CONSIDER ABOUT SEMINARY

Appendix 1

Seminary Past and Present

Theological Teaching and Learning

In this book we have discussed as much about theological education as is probably healthy! I have thus included this portion of the book about the past and present of seminary in an appendix. And although there will definitely be many people who will not care as much about the history of seminary, there will likewise be many people who will. Accordingly, I would like to continue our discussion about seminary education in this book by retelling very briefly the history of seminaries. This is because the history of seminaries is a highly suspenseful story full of intrigue, deception, and even murder. All right, maybe I'm fibbing a little—but it *is* interesting! I will pick up the story of seminaries in the early church before concluding with some thoughts on contemporary seminaries.

Theological Education and the Rise of the European University

The seminary as we know it today is two hundred years old. It is a markedly American phenomenon in the sense that the structures of most seminaries in North America have connections to the original Protestant seminaries in the nineteenth century. Because this book is interested primarily in seminary, and not Christian education in its own right, we are not going to spend much time talking about Christian education before the birth of the seminary. However, I would like to highlight minimally the training that some Christian professionals received prior to seminaries before discussing the rise of the seminary as well as theological education today.

Perhaps the greatest educational development during the Middle Ages was the university.

Although there were specific types of schools available for a select number of individuals in the first few centuries of the church, the concept of a seminary as we think about it did not exist for hundreds of years. During the eleventh and twelfth centuries, there developed in Europe a new form of education—one that witnessed great popularity then and one that continues to this day: the university. Although the vast majority of the great theologians that we know of today from the medieval period usually attended (and eventually taught at) universities, there were still many priests who never did so. For this reason, we must keep in mind that—though the university was important to the theological formation of future priests and theologians—the typical priest or other Christian minister did not have a university education.

Theological Education in the Modern Church

The founding of universities in the medieval church has been one of the most enduring and important developments of the past millennium. Once they were founded it became common for certain prospective ministers to earn a university degree before entering a more specialized field of study in theology—especially as the centuries passed and a university education became more accessible. Oftentimes this more specialized field of study was conducted at the university in the form of a graduate degree. At other times university graduates become apprentices to practicing ministers to learn the trade of pastoral ministry. This was especially the case within certain theological traditions in England and colonial America. In fact, it was not until the sixteenth century that seminaries were officially created, and it was not until the nineteenth century that the current model for seminary education was instituted. Before then future clergymen (still no women yet) did as best as they could to secure appropriate theological and pastoral instruction.

It was not until the nineteenth century in New England that the current model for seminary education was instituted.

The Founding of Catholic Seminaries in Europe

The sixteenth century was one of the most theologically tumultuous centuries of the Christian era. All across Europe thousands of Christians officially protested against the Catholic Church and ultimately divided from it, becoming what are known today as Protestants ("Protesters"). Partly in reaction to the Protestant movement and partly as a result of desiring reform, the Catholic Church convened a special council around the middle of the sixteenth century to discuss important issues related to Catholicism. It was called the Council of Trent, and it produced a series of canons or decrees about Catholic doctrine that gave direction to the Catholic Church for centuries.

The Council of Trent in the sixteenth century founded the first seminaries in Europe.

For our purposes, the most important canon that the council produced was the creation of seminaries, which they referred to as "perpetual nurseries [seminaries] of ministers." These seminaries or theological nurseries were designed to instruct prospective priests and other young ministerial candidates by offering practical knowledge about the ministry and theology. We have to remember that up to this time clerical education had been very basic and many priests were regularly without a university education. Consequently, the creation of the seminary was designed to counter clerical under-education and to provide quality theological and practical instruction for future priests.

The Founding of Colleges in America

Although the term "seminary" was largely created in the sixteenth century by the Catholic Church, the model for seminary education today stems largely from the American university. For this reason, we will briefly discuss the formation of the first (Protestant) universities in America before then discussing the creation of the theological seminary of the nineteenth century—which was based upon the American university.

The first university founded in the United States was Harvard College in 1636 with the "training of clergy" as one of its primary purposes. Although Harvard was not officially a seminary (the divinity school was added in the early 1800s), theological training was minimally integrated into the curriculum along with a more classical education (conducted in Latin of course). Historically all students studied divinity on Saturdays—usually under the instruction of the college president. It is estimated that in the sixteenth century a little more than half of the graduates of Harvard entered the ministry. Those who entered the ministry usually followed one of two different paths after graduating from college (though some followed both paths): apprenticeship and/or earning a graduate degree.

Apprenticeship to Practicing Ministers

Because colleges in America were largely based upon universities in Europe, the curriculum which students studied was quite theoretical and intellectual. Therefore, students intent on the ministry were in need of practical experience and training after college before they became pastors of individual churches.

Before seminaries became professionalized and standardized, most pastors had to apprentice themselves to older pastors.

One common way that they gained this practical training was by residing with a practicing minister for several months to several years where they "read divinity," that is, where they compiled a reading list of important theological works and studied them on a practical level under the direction of mentors and ministers. Students read these books, discussed them with their mentors, and taught and preached occasionally. Sometimes one pastor would take on several students at the same time—creating a miniature divinity school referred to at times as "the schools of the prophets." This model of apprenticeship was very common in colonial America and continued until around the nineteenth century.

Earning a Graduate Degree (Related to Divinity)

The other way that ministers received practical training after college was by enrolling in a master's degree (there were no earned doctoral degrees in colonial America). Students who enrolled in this degree typically chose an area of study—for our purposes, divinity—and spent the next two or three years reading and learning about divinity under the supervision of the college president or other competent tutor (at this time—unlike today—college presidents were usually clergymen and they were largely responsible for the theological education of their students). The tradition of these two approaches to the ministry—apprenticeship and/or a master's degree—continued until around the nineteenth century. After this time professional education in America went through considerable change and development.

The Founding of (Protestant) Seminaries

The first (Protestant) theological seminary to offer graduate instruction in the United States was Andover Seminary in Massachusetts. Classes formally began in the fall of 1808. Although Andover was not technically the first institution that provided theological education in America, it has the distinction of being the first graduate school of theological education. (The first American Catholic seminary was St. Mary's in Baltimore, founded in 1791.) Andover Seminary was the first institution that provided several specialized faculty members, a sizable library with a handsome endowment, and a very specific three-year curriculum. It was also the first seminary that mandated a bachelor's degree from college for admittance (or at least the passing of an examination in Greek, Latin, and the sciences!).

This pattern of seminary education and curriculum has remained to the present, and little has changed with regard to the curricular division that Andover pioneered of biblical studies, theology, as well as church history and (eventually) practical theology. As a result of Andover's success, several other universities began adding divinity schools, and many other independent seminaries were additionally created. Harvard was the first to do so, in 1811, by appending a divinity school to the college. Within a year Princeton Theological Seminary was founded as an independent seminary. Yale added its divinity school to the college shortly thereafter, as numerous other seminaries were inaugurated as well.

Andover Seminary was the first seminary of graduate theological instruction. Classes began in the fall of 1808.

By the 1860s theological seminaries had increased exponentially. This increase in seminaries was largely inspired by religious awakenings and political and social controversies, as well as the rise of many new denominations. It was also around this time that seminaries experienced another important development in theological education: the development of theological scholarship. Seminaries became very specialized, and the ideal of scholarship transformed the seminary from one of practical concerns to one of intellectual concerns as well. Throughout the remainder of the nineteenth century as well as the twentieth century, seminaries multiplied across North America in both diversity and sheer size and grandeur.

Seminaries in the Twenty-First Century

There are currently more than 250 seminaries in North America accredited by the Association of Theological Schools, as well as countless others that are not accredited. This is quite a change from the nineteenth century! In the United States and Canada, seminaries are well represented throughout all geographical areas. What is more, with the addition of online

----

Seminaries today can be described in one word—diversity.

learning, distance education, and satellite campuses, there is a seminary within reach of almost anyone in North America. But if I had to describe seminaries today in one word, I would probably use the word *diversity*. There is more diversity at seminaries these days than ever before. In this section I draw attention to some of the ways that seminaries today differ from previous schools: in diversity of programs, ethnicity, gender, and career prospects.

Program (Degree) Diversity

As I noted earlier, most students who went to seminary before the middle of the twentieth century either entered pastoral ministry or pursued something similar: missions or teaching. The past several decades, however, have witnessed a great increase in the number of students who are not entering pastoral ministry or missions, or even teaching. These students are pursuing a variety of professions upon graduation from seminary—whether in the ministry or otherwise. As a result of the evolving interests and aspirations of many seminarians, seminaries have evolved as well. One way in particular that they have done so has to do with the variety of programs offered these days. It is not an exaggeration to say that there are dozens of different degrees and programs that seminaries now provide their students. These programs are extremely wide-ranging, from the traditional master of divinity to the ubiquitous and eclectic master of arts. You can study anything from administration to communications to leadership to music to theology. And although it is difficult to know for sure, I am of the opinion that seminary programs will become even more diverse and eclectic in the next few decades.

In many seminaries today you could study anything from administration to communications to leadership to music to theology.

Ethnic Diversity

The traditional seminary in North America was one filled almost exclusively with Caucasians. Over the years this has begun to change with the growing diversity in the United States and in Canada. More and more students from nontraditional backgrounds are pursuing a theological education, and there is thus more ethnic diversity in seminaries these days than ever before. In fact, this diversity is only expected to increase.

Gender Diversity

The rise in the number of women who attend seminaries today is notable. According to the Association of Theological Schools, around 36 percent of all seminarians are female (www.ats.edu). In fact, it is common these days to find women represented at more than the student level: many faculty members at seminaries are women, and there are several female seminary presidents and administrators as well. These trends will undoubtedly continue to increase in the ensuing decades, and more and more seminaries will produce female graduates who will pursue careers related to the ministry.

Age Diversity

Aside from the increase in the number of women represented at seminary—both as faculty and as students—there is also great diversity of age at seminary. Although seminaries have always had their fair share of diversity in this respect, many schools today have students of various ages. In fact, you are just as likely to run into a student of fifty as you are one of twenty-five. There are students of all ages—students in their sixties and even seventies; as a result, I am pretty confident that you will be able to find many people similar to your age at seminary—regardless of how young or old you are.

Career Diversity

The last feature of educational diversity that we will discuss is related to diversity in age: career diversity. By career diversity I mean students of different backgrounds as well as students who are pursuing different careers. Part of the reason for the diversity in ages at seminary is that many students are second-career students, that is, students who are moving from one career (usually a secular one) to another (usually to full-time Christian ministry). I remember two of the first students that I met while in seminary: one was a podiatrist and the other had been in computer software for many years. The first student was married with no children and was attending seminary to become an educated layperson, while the other student had several older children and was seeking ordained ministry. I, on the other hand, was in my early twenties and pursuing a career related to teaching. It was wonderful to be around such diversity, as each of us was able to learn from the others. After graduation each of us pursued very different career paths: one is a pastor; another is a layperson; and the third is a sort of seminary vagabond!

The New Seminary

We have discussed some of the changes in seminary education over the past couple of hundred years. In contrast to seminaries in the nineteenth and even the twentieth century, schools today are more diverse and accessible. Seminary education presumably will only continue to become more so. For the most part, this is good news for you, because it means that you will be eligible for and represented at seminary regardless of age, ethnicity, or gender; and you will also be able to find a program that fits well with your schedule, regardless of location, job, or time commitment. This is indeed an exciting time go to seminary. Maybe I can talk my wife into my earning my fourth seminary degree, after all!

Seminary Checklists

Guide to Using the Following Charts

The following charts contain checklists for some of the most important decisions that you will have to make when it comes to seminary. Each of them is contained in some form or another within the different chapters of this book. Be sure to consult the specific chapters for questions and topics to reflect on when it comes to many of the important decisions that you will have to make before, during, and even after seminary.

Discerning Whether to Attend Seminary

Deciding whether to attend seminary is one of the most important decisions you will make when it comes to your profession. I hope that you will find the following checklist helpful; it is designed to help you think through this decision. Consider it prayerfully and with pen in hand.

_____ I have prayed and thought about this decision fervently

_____ My congregation has confirmed this decision

_____ My immediate family (spouse, children) support my decision

_____ I have the time and money needed to attend seminary

_____ I have the right temperament, ability, and interest

_____ I want to dedicate my life to serving God and others

_____ I am ready to dedicate several years of my life to seminary

_____ I want to learn more about the Bible and theology

_____ I want to enter a career related to the church and ministry

_____ I cannot explain it, but I believe that I am led to go to seminary

Deciding What Factors to Consider before Seminary

There are countless factors to consider when it comes to deciding what type of seminary you will attend. The following checklist includes what I have found to be most crucial for many students. Due to the great variety of seminaries today—remember that there are more than 250 seminaries accredited by ATS in North America—you are able to be as specific and detailed as you would like when choosing the right school for your circumstances.

_____ I want to attend an ATS-accredited seminary

_____ I want to attend a university-based divinity/theological school

_____ I want to attend a freestanding seminary

_____ I want to attend a seminary in my immediate area

_____ I don't care whether the seminary is located out of state

_____ The type of degree I am seeking is found at most every school

_____ I am seeking a degree that is very specialized

_____ I need to attend a school that assists students seeking licensure

_____ I need to find and enroll in a program that has distance education

_____ I need to be sensitive to my financial situation while in seminary

_____ I want to attend a school where I know someone (teacher, student)

_____ I need to find a school that is affiliated with my denomination

_____ The theological affiliation of the school is not important to me

Determining What Degree to Earn

If you are going to enroll in a more traditional program, the type of school you attend should not have any effect on you; however, if you are searching for a more specialized degree, you may need to decide on a degree before deciding on a school. As I explained in the body of the book, there are two kinds of degree programs, basic or first-professional degrees and advanced or graduate degrees. You will have to enroll in a basic degree if you have never attended seminary before, and you will probably enroll in a graduate degree if you have previously graduated from seminary. To make things easier, I will divide these two types of degrees into two separate charts. For basic degrees, consult the first chart; see the second one for advanced degrees. The following, however, are not exhaustive.

Basic or First-Professional Programs and Degrees

____ Master of Divinity

____ Master of Arts

____ Master of Theological Studies

____ Master of Religious Education

____ Master of (Church) Music

Advanced or Graduate Programs and Degrees

____ Master of (Sacred) Theology

____ Doctor of Ministry

____ Doctor of Theology

____ Doctor of Philosophy

____ Doctor of Education

____ Doctor of Missiology

____ Doctor of Musical Arts

Discovering a Profession after Graduation

It is never too early to begin thinking about what profession you will pursue after graduating from seminary. This chart allows you to highlight professions of interest. Check as many as apply. Throughout seminary pray for guidance and speak with your faith community and friends about possible career opportunities.

____ I want to be a pastor or priest

____ I want to be a (Christian) counselor or therapist

____ I want to be a primary or secondary teacher (at a Christian school)

_____ I want to be a college or seminary professor

_____ I want to be a Christian speaker or preacher

_____ I want to be a missionary or church planter (domestic or international)

_____ I want to be a chaplain (in the military, at a university, at a retirement home)

_____ I want to be involved in Christian music or worship (at church or a school)

_____ I want to be a biblical translator

_____ I want to be an administrator (at a Christian school or organization)

_____ I want to be a Christian author

_____ I want to work at a parachurch organization (discipleship, evangelism)

_____ I want to work in communications and media in relation to the church

_____ I have a specific profession in mind not on this list

Appendix 3

Glossary of Theological Terms

Accreditation: Standard requirements set by an organization—for our purposes, the Association of Theological Schools—and accountability to this organization and other accredited schools for the quality of education.

Association of Theological Schools (ATS): Organization that monitors and enhances seminary education. In this book, only seminaries accredited by ATS are considered.

AD/BC: The abbreviations AD (*Anno Domini*—in the year of the Lord [Latin]) and BC (Before Christ) have been replaced in all secular and many religious circles with BCE (Before the Common Era) and CE (Common Era), respectively, to neutralize the religious implications and remove any Christian imperialism.

Atonement: Theological concept that Jesus's death on the cross appeases or satisfies God's wrath against humanity.

Augustine: North African bishop and church theologian (354–430). He is regarded as one of the most important church theologians in the history of the church.

Baptist: Protestant denomination, receiving its name as a result of its emphasis on believer's baptism instead of paedobaptism (infant baptism); Baptists are also usually characterized by their belief in the free will of the believer.

Baptism: One of the two principal sacraments of the Protestant church. It comes from a Greek work that refers to "being dipped in water." Apart from agreeing that it plays an important part in the life of the church and the believer, churches often disagree on how to perform it: at birth or in adulthood, by immersion or by pouring.

Biblical studies: One of the four traditional disciplines offered at seminary. This discipline includes all those courses related to the Bible (Old Testament and

New Testament). Every seminary degree contains a portion of coursework dedicated to biblical studies.

Canon: This comes from a Greek term meaning "reed," which was used as a measuring device. It formally became the term that standardized and recognized a number of books that are holy to the Christian community.

Chaplain: A minister (pastor or priest) who leads and serves those outside the church. Chaplains often work in the military, at a hospital, or in some related setting.

Christocentric: Centered on Christ, or Jesus. The term is often used when interpreting the Bible and when speaking about theology in general.

Church history/Historical theology: One of the four traditional seminary disciplines. It concentrates on persons, events, and dates within the history of the church. When the two are distinguished, church history focuses on examining history from the church's perspective, while historical theology focuses on theology from a historical perspective.

Circa: A Latin word that means "around," used mostly with dates—abbreviated ca.

Clergy: A person who is ordained in the Christian church.

Divinity: A more traditional term for Christian theology. In seminary, there are a couple of main usages of this term. First, many seminaries that are affiliated with a denomination and are part of a university are traditionally called "divinity schools." Second, the most common degree offered at seminaries is called the master of divinity.

Doctor of ministry (DMin): This is essentially the doctoral equivalent of the master of divinity. Though a doctoral degree, it is focused on ministry, in contrast to a ThD or PhD, which is focused more on teaching and research. The DMin is most appropriate for those who have already earned the master of divinity and who need more specialized instruction on topics related to the ministry. It is ideal for practicing pastors who require more education (for a variety of reasons) or for those who want to teach more practical or ministry-related courses at the college or seminary level.

Doctor of philosophy (PhD): Highest degree offered at seminaries. It requires the master of divinity or master of arts for admittance, and is the appropriate degree for those who want to teach and do research at the college or seminary level. It is a rigorous and time-consuming degree and will take several years to complete. There are several stages to earning this degree—passing language exams, taking classes, passing written and oral exams, and writing an original dissertation of several hundred pages.

Doctor of theology (ThD): This degree is virtually identical to the PhD, and most seminaries that offered this degree have changed its name to PhD. Perhaps the only distinction between the two is that a ThD is more specifically related to the church than is the PhD. However, the requirements for this degree are identical to those of the PhD. At the seminary level, the ThD and PhD are equivalent; the first is the traditional term, while the second is the more common term today.

Doctrine: From the Latin word for "teaching," refers to central beliefs and convictions of the Christian church with regard to faith.

Ecclesial: Pertaining to the church (from the Greek word meaning "church"). Related words are *ecclesiology* (study of church governance) and *ecclesiastical* (referring to the church).

Ecclesiology: The study of church governance; or the doctrine of the church (coming from the Greek [and Latin] word for "church").

Election: A theological doctrine that refers to God's choosing or election of a person to receive salvation and become part of the church.

Emergent/Emerging/Missional church: All refer to roughly the same thing, a diverse group of committed Christians who seek to reexamine Christianity in light of contemporary culture and to more seriously engage the postmodern culture in which the church finds itself. Takes serious authenticity and spirituality in the Christian life, and is conversational rather than confrontational (with those both in and outside the church).

Eucharist: Also called "communion" or "the Lord's Supper." It comes from a Greek word meaning "to give thanks."

Exegesis: Coming from a Greek word "to explain"; in technical theological terms, it refers to the act of interpreting and expounding the meaning and message of a text, most usually the Bible. In seminary, students often write what are called "exegetical papers," that is, research papers on a particular passage of the Bible intended to explain the original context, history, and meaning.

Exile: Refers to the time period when the Israelites were conquered by the Babylonians and exiled there in 587 BC (and early 600s) and continuing thereafter for 70 years. The return from exile, the restoration, occurred in ca. 515 BC.

Fall: The fall refers to when Adam and Eve succumbed to temptation and sin in Genesis 2–3. According to the apostle Paul, "just as sin came into the world through one man [Adam], and death came through sin [his eating of the prohibited tree], and so death spread to all because all have sinned" (Rom. 5:12 NRSV).

Hebrew Scriptures: A common and more sensitive way to designate the Old Testament. Some argue, for instance, that the term "old" in the Old Testament connotes that which is obsolete or inferior. The term "Hebrew Scriptures" does not offend non-Christians, so it is used instead.

Hermeneutics: Stemming from the Greek word that means "to interpret," it is regarded as the art and science of biblical interpretation.

Intertestamental: Time period between the Hebrew Scriptures and the New Testament, dating roughly from 400 BC to 50 AD. This time period produced extremely important documents written by the (Jewish) religious community before the time of Jesus.

Justification: The doctrine of how one becomes a Christian or is made right by God.

Layperson: The opposite of clergyperson. This is simply a person who is not a professional minister or one who works in any ministerial capacity. Instead, it is a person who serves the church as a volunteer (Sunday school teacher, deacon, and so forth) because he or she works in a secular profession. Many seminary graduates today are laypersons instead of clergypersons.

Levites: The priestly tribe out of the twelve nations originally fathered by Jacob/Israel. The Levites were the tribe that supervised the religious or liturgical aspects of Israel's religious life. In Christian terms, the Levites were the priests or pastors of Israel's congregations.

Liturgy: Worship pattern or ceremony of the church. This term is usually applied to more historic churches, such as the Catholic church or the Anglican church.

Lutheran: A Protestant that traces his or her history and theology to the Protestant reformer Martin Luther (1483–1546), whose bedrock conviction of "justification by faith alone" became the emblem of the Protestant Reformation.

Master of arts: This is a basic degree offered at seminary. It is either more academic or more ministerial in nature. It is usually completed in two to three years, full-time. There are dozens of specializations possible with this degree. It is most appropriate for those who will not pursue pastoral ministry.

Master of divinity: The classic and most common degree offered at seminary. It is a ministerial degree, which is designed to encompass most career prospects for professional Christian ministry. It is usually completed in three to four years full time. It is ideal for those who will pursue pastoral ministry, and it is probably the degree to enroll in if a student is not sure what to study while in seminary.

Master of (sacred) theology: A graduate degree offered at seminary. It usually requires the master of divinity for admittance and will take one to two years full time. It offers students more advanced training in theology and was traditionally the degree that many sought before enrolling in a doctoral program. Sometimes the adjective "sacred" is used to refer to this degree, with almost no distinction if it is not added.

Mennonite: A Protestant that traces his or her history to Menno Simons (1496–1561); otherwise known as Anabaptists, which is a Greek term that means "to rebaptize." Mennonites were given this name because they rejected infant baptism; they also oppose war and tend to live apart from the rest of the culture.

Middle Ages: Time period roughly between St. Augustine or Gregory the Great and Martin Luther, that is, between ca. AD 500 and 1500.

Minister: Literally, "one who serves," a minister is a clergyperson in the church. It is sometimes synonymous with the words *pastor* or *priest*.

Ministry/Ministerial: Serving and building up the church. Usually those in the ministry are full-time servants of the church—ministers, missionaries, educators, and so on.

Monasticism: A theological development that arose in the third and fourth centuries AD. It is characterized by solitude (whether in a community or alone), prayer, contemplation, study, physical labor, and worship.

Montanism: A Christian movement around the middle of the second century that stressed the dominance of the Holy Spirit, so called after one of its advocates, Montanus.

Ordination: The act of dedicating to the church an individual who has undergone extensive training and evaluation. Ordination allows a person to administer the sacraments, preach, lead worship, and perform other ecclesial functions.

Original sin: Refers to the disobedience of Adam and Eve in Genesis 3, as well as to how sin is transmitted from generation to generation.

Parachurch: An organization that exists alongside the church but is itself not a church. It is a type of Christian ministry that works along with the local church in establishing and maintaining Christianity.

Pastor: Literally, "shepherd," *pastor* is a common term for a priest or a minister. This term is often used by Protestants to refer to one who is ordained to lead the church, in contrast to the term *priest*, which is often used by Catholics and Anglicans.

Pentateuch: Refers to the first five book of the Old Testament, traditionally believed to be composed by Moses: Genesis, Exodus, Leviticus, Numbers, and Deuteronomy. This is also referred to as the Torah.

Patriarchs: From the Greek word for "father." These are the foundational (male) figures of the Book of Genesis, with whom God made covenant promises. Abraham, Isaac, and Jacob are considered the principal patriarchs.

Pneumatology: The doctrine of the Holy Spirit. This comes from the Greek word that means "spirit" in the New Testament. It is a topic discussed under systematic theology.

Practical theology: One of the four traditional disciplines offered at seminary. Practical theology focuses on more practical matters related to theology, such as counseling, preaching, spirituality, evangelism, and pastoral care.

Predestination: The belief that God chooses who will be saved before that person is even born.

Premillennial: Meaning "before the millennium," that is, with reference to Jesus's bodily return to the world at the end of the ages. The concept stemmed largely from the theology of Irishman J. Nelson Darby (1800–1882), who modified earlier premillennial views and whose followers popularized it, especially in America during the early twentieth century. When coupled with the teachings of the Scofield Bible of the twentieth century, premillennialism became very popular. Premillennialism is characterized as believing that Jesus will return to rule in Jerusalem for exactly 1,000 years before seven years of chaos for unbelievers, based on literal readings from the books of Daniel and Revelation.

Presbyterian: A Protestant denomination that traces its history primarily to John Calvin (1509–1560); Presbyterianism is characterized by having a strong church hierarchy (which is the meaning of the Greek term), predestination, and God's sovereignty. Presbyterianism was popular in Scotland, and its popularity influenced both England and colonial America.

Priest: One who is commissioned or ordained to lead a specific congregation, preach, administer the sacraments, lead, and officiate at weddings and funerals. Priests are sometimes regarded as synonymous with pastors and ministers; the only difference is that priests are often Catholic or Anglican, whereas pastors are often Protestants.

Reformation: Initially intended to "reform" the (Catholic) church, the Protestant Reformation eventuated into the greatest church split of all times. It is considered a protest against what were conceived as harmful and unbiblical practices of the Catholic church. Martin Luther's posting of his Ninety-five Theses on the church door in Wittenberg on October 31, 1517, is usually regarded as the beginning of the Reformation.

Reformed: Protestant tradition that traces its history to Ulrich Zwingli (1484–1531) and John Calvin (1509–1564). People in the Reformed tradition are also often called Calvinists. Hallmarks include the sovereignty of God, predestination, and the centrality of the Holy Spirit in the life of the believer.

Sacrament: A visible manifestation of an invisible reality. All major divisions of the church agree on the twin sacraments of baptism and communion. The Catholic church, however, identifies five more sacraments than does Protestantism.

Sanctification: In theology the doctrine of how one remains holy throughout one's lifetime. It is often put in relation to justification. The term comes from a Latin word that refers to holiness or being set aside for God.

Scribe: Jewish scholar who was trained in reading and writing during biblical times. Scribes were responsible for copying and preserving the Bible as well as being the principal interpreters of it. They were like lawyers of the Bible.

Sectarian: Neutral with regard to religious affiliation—neither affirming nor denying any particular religious expression. It is distinct from secular schools in the sense that sectarians are religious people who simply favor one form of religious expression over another, while seculars are purely nonreligious.

Seminary: School of graduate theological education that expressly prepares students for careers related to ministry and the Christian church that offers master's and doctoral degrees.

Systematic theology: The systematic ordering of the Christian faith. It is one of the four traditional disciplines of seminary curriculum.

Sovereignty: Refers to God's complete authority and transcendence over creation.

Soteriology: The study of salvation, that is, how one becomes saved or justified.

Temple: The temple was central to Judaism. King Solomon built the first one, which was destroyed around 586 BC by the Babylonians. It was rebuilt less than a hundred years later but did not attain its former glory. The second temple was destroyed by the Romans in AD 70. It has never been rebuilt.

Theodicy: Reconciling God's goodness to the effects of sin and suffering in this world.

Theology: Study of God. Comes from the Greek word for God (*theos*). Theology is the catchall expression for studying divine things—whether the Bible, church history, or ethics. Theology is the principal field of study at seminaries.

Theological school/School of theology: Another name for a seminary. Traditionally, theological schools were nondenominational seminaries affiliated with universities. In this book, a theological school is synonymous with a divinity school, and it is simply a more specific name for a seminary in general. Schools of theology are affiliated with universities.

Theosis: In the Orthodox church, the doctrine of how one becomes more holy and more closely connected to God over time.

Torah: A Hebrew word usually translated as "law" or "instruction." The Torah also refers to the first five books of the Old Testament: Genesis, Exodus, Leviticus, Numbers, and Deuteronomy. In this sense, it is synonymous with the term *Pentateuch*.

Trinity: Refers to the Christian belief that God exists in three persons: Father, Son, and Holy Spirit. At the same time, however, God is still one. This term was first used in the early Christian church, and it has been a cardinal doctrine of the church since then.

Worldview: Coming originally from the German word *Weltanschauung*, it refers to the totality of a system's beliefs about the world that shape how it thinks, understands, believes, and functions.

Yahweh: Covenant name of God in the Old Testament. Its etymology is not certain, but it most likely is related to the verb "to be." Hence, the name could mean something like "I am who I am" or "I will be who I will be." It emphasizes God's eternity and constant presence or being. The name "Jehovah" is now known to be a mispronunciation of the name Yahweh.

Bibliography

Works Cited

Arndt, Johann. *True Christianity*. Classics of Western Spirituality. New York: Paulist Press, 1979.

Bonhoeffer, Dietrich. *Ethics*. New York: Collier Books, 1955.

Brushaber, George. "The Twenty-first Century Seminary." *Christianity Today*, May 17, 1993, 45–46.

Campolo, Tony, and Brian McLaren. *Adventures in Missing the Point: How the Culture-Controlled Church Neutered the Gospel*. Grand Rapids: Zondervan/Youth Specialties, 2003.

Canons and Decrees of the Council of Trent. Edited by H. J. Schroeder. St. Louis: B. Herder, 1955.

Ebeling, Gerhard. *The Word of God and Tradition: Historical Studies Interpreting the Divisions of Christianity*. Translated by S. H. Hooke. Philadelphia: Fortress Press, 1968.

Gore, Charles. *The Church and the Ministry*. London: Longmans, Green, 1919.

Lewis, C. S. *The Weight of Glory and Other Addresses*. New York: HarperCollins, 2001.

Luther, Martin. *The Large Catechism of Martin Luther*. Translated by Robert Fischer. Philadelphia: Fortress, 1990.

———. *Luther's Works*. Vol. 36. Minneapolis: Fortress Press, 1959.

Muller, Richard. *The Study of Theology: From Biblical Interpretation to Contemporary Formulation*. Grand Rapids: Zondervan, 1991.

Oden, Thomas. *Pastoral Theology: Essentials of Ministry*. San Francisco: HarperSanFrancisco, 1983.

Southern, R. W. *Western Society and the Church in the Middle Ages*. Penguin History of the Church. London: Penguin Books, 1970.

Warfield, B. B. *The Religious Life of the Theological Student*. Edited by John E. Meeter. Nutley, NJ: Presbyterian and Refomed Publishing, [1970–1977?]. Delivered by Dr. Warfield at Princeton Theological Seminary on October 4, 1911.

Webster, John. *Holy Scripture: A Dogmatic Sketch*. Cambridge: Cambridge University Press, 2003.

Wesley, John. *John and Charles Wesley: Selected Prayers, Hymns, Journal Notes, Sermons, Letters, and Treatises*. Edited by Frank Whaling. Classics of Western Spirituality. New York: Paulist Press, 1981.

Willimon, William. *Calling and Character: Virtues of the Ordained Life*. Nashville: Abingdon, 2000.

Wright, N. T. *The New Testament and the People of God*. Minneapolis: Fortress Press, 1992.

Organizations Cited

Association of Theological Schools, www.ats.edu

American Counselors Association, www.counseling.org

American Psychological Association, www.apa.org

National Board for Certified Counselors, www.nbcc.org

Presbyterian Church (U.S.A.), www.pcusa.org

Seminaries Cited

Alliance Theological Seminary, www.alliance.edu

Andover Newton Theological School, www.ants.edu

Asbury Theological Seminary, www.asburyseminary.edu

Ashland Theological Seminary, www.ashland.edu/seminary

Associated Mennonite Biblical Seminary, www.ambs.edu

Aquinas Institute of Theology, www.ai.edu

Atlantic School of Theology, www.astheology.ns.ca

Bangor Theological Seminary, www.bts.edu

Beeson Divinity School of Samford University, www.beesondivinity.com

Bethel Seminary of Bethel University, http://seminary.bethel.edu

Biblical Theological Seminary, www.biblical.edu

Boston University School of Theology, www.bu.edu/sth

Brite Divinity School of Texas Christian University, www.brite.tcu.edu

Calvin Theological Seminary, www.calvinseminary.edu

Campbell University Divinity School, www.campbell.edu/divinity

Candler School of Theology of Emory University, www.candler.emory.edu

Capital Bible Seminary of Washington Bible College, www.bible.edu

Catholic University School of Theology and Religious Studies, www.religiousstudies.cua.edu

Chicago Theological Seminary, www.ctschicago.edu

Christian Theological Seminary, www.cts.edu

Church of God Theological Seminary, www.cogts.edu

Claremont School of Theology, www.cst.edu

Columbia International University Seminary and School of Missions, www.ciu.edu/seminary

Columbia Theological Seminary, www.ctsnet.edu

Concordia Seminary, www.csl.edu

Covenant Theological Seminary, www.covenantseminary.edu

Dallas Theological Seminary, www.dts.edu

Denver Seminary, www.denverseminary.edu

Drew University Theological School, www.drew.edu/theo.aspx

Duke University Divinity School, www.divinity.duke.edu

Eden Theological Seminary, www.eden.edu

Erskine Theological Seminary, www.erskineseminary.org

Evangelical School of Theology, www.evangelical.edu

Fuller Theological Seminary, www.fuller.edu

General Theological Seminary, www.gts.edu

George Fox Evangelical Seminary of George Fox University, www.georgefox.edu/seminary

Golden Gate Baptist Theological Seminary, www.ggbts.edu

Gordon-Conwell Theological Seminary, www.gcts.edu

Graduate Theological Union, www.gtu.edu

Grand Rapids Theological Seminary of Cornerstone University, http://grts.cornerstone.edu

Haggard School of Theology of Azusa Pacific University, www.apu.edu/theology

Hartford Seminary, www.hartsem.edu

Harvard Divinity School of Harvard University, www.hds.harvard.edu

Holy Cross Greek Orthodox School of Theology, www.hchc.edu

Howard University Divinity School, www.howard.edu/divinity

Iliff School of Theology, www.iliff.edu

Interdenominational Theological Center, www.itc.edu

Lexington Theological Seminary, www.lextheo.edu

Louisville Presbyterian Theological Seminary, www.lpts.edu

Lutheran Theological Seminary at Gettysburg, www.ltsg.edu

Lutheran Theological Seminary in Philadelphia, www.ltsp.edu

Knox Theological Seminary, www.knoxseminary.edu

Mars Hill Graduate School, www.mhgs.edu

McCormick Theological Seminary, www.mccormick.edu

Memphis Theological Seminary, www.memphisseminary.edu

Mennonite Brethren Biblical Seminary, www.mbseminary.edu

Midwestern Baptist Theological Seminary, www.mbts.edu

Moravian Theological Seminary, www.moravianseminary.edu

Multnomah Biblical Seminary, www.multnomah.edu/seminary

Mundelein Seminary of the University of St. Mary of the Lake, www.usml.edu

Nazarene Theological Seminary, www.nts.edu

Newman Theological College, www.newman.edu

New Brunswick Theological Seminary, www.nbts.edu

New Orleans Baptist Theological Seminary, www.nobts.edu

North Park Theological Seminary, www.northpark.edu/sem

Oral Roberts School of Theology, www.oru.edu

Perkins School of Theology of Southern Methodist University, www.smu.edu/
     theology

Phoenix Seminary, www.phoenixseminary.edu

Phillips Theological Seminary, www.ptstulsa.edu

Pittsburgh Theological Seminary, www.pts.edu

Princeton Theological Seminary, www.ptsem.edu

Providence Theological Seminary, http://prov.ca

Reformed Episcopal Seminary, www.reseminary.edu

Reformed Theological Seminary, www.rts.edu

Regent College, www.regent-college.edu

Regent University School of Divinity, www.regent.edu/acad/schdiv

Sacred Heart Major Seminary, www.aodonline.org/SHMS/SHMS.htm

San Francisco Theological Seminary, www.sfts.edu

Seventh-day Adventist Theological Seminary of Andrews University, www.an-
     drews.edu/SEM

Southeastern Baptist Theological Seminary, www.sebts.edu

Southern Baptist Theological Seminary, www.sbts.edu

Southwestern Baptist Theological Seminary, www.swbts.edu

St. Augustine's Seminary, www.staugustines.on.ca

St. Charles Borromeo Seminary, www.scs.edu

St. Mary's Seminary and University, www.stmarys.edu

St. Tikhon's Orthodox Theological Seminary, www.stots.edu

St. Vladimir's Theological Seminary, www.svots.edu

Talbot School of Theology of Biola University, www.talbot.edu

Trinity Evangelical Divinity School of Trinity International University, www.tiu.
edu/divinity

Trinity Lutheran Seminary, www.trinitylutheranseminary.edu

Union Theological Seminary, www.utsnyc.edu

Union Theological Seminary and Presbyterian School of Christian Education,
www.union-psce.edu

United Theological Seminary, www.united.edu

University of Chicago Divinity School, http://divinity.uchicago.edu

University of Notre Dame Department of Theology, http://theology.nd.edu

University of the South School of Theology, http://theology.sewanee.edu

University of St. Thomas School of Theology, www.stthom.edu

Vanderbilt University Divinity School, www.vanderbilt.edu/divinity

Virginia Theological Seminary, www.vts.edu

Wake Forest University Divinity School, http://divinity/wfu.edu

Wartburg Theological Seminary, www.wartburgseminary.edu

Washington Theological Union, www.wtu.edu

Wesley Theological Seminary, www.wesleyseminary.edu

Western Seminary, www.westernseminary.edu

Western Theological Seminary, www.westernsem.edu

Westminster Seminary of California, www.wscal.edu

Westminster Theological Seminary, www.wts.edu

Weston Jesuit School of Theology, www.wjst.edu

Yale Divinity School of Yale University, www.yale.edu/divinity

Brazos Press is grounded in the ancient, ecumenical Christian tradition, understood as living and dynamic. As legend has it, Brazos is the Spanish name explorers gave to a prominent Texas river upon seeing how its winding waters sustained fertile soil in an arid land. They christened this life-giving channel Los Brazos de Dios, "the arms of God."

Our logo connotes a river with multiple currents all flowing in the same direction, just as the major streams of the Christian tradition are various but all surging from and to the same God. The logo's three "streams" also reflect the Trinitarian God who lives and gives life at the heart of all true Christian faith.

Our books are marketed and distributed intensively and broadly through the American Booksellers Association and the Christian Booksellers networks and bookstores; national chains and independent bookstores; Catholic and mainline bookstores; and library and international markets. We are a division of Baker Publishing Group.

Brazos Book Club and Border Crossings

Brazos books help people grapple with the important issues of the day and make Christian sense of pervasive issues in the church, academy, and contemporary world. Our authors engage such topics as spirituality, the arts, the economy, popular culture, theology, biblical studies, the social sciences, and more. At both the popular and academic levels, we publish books by evangelical, Roman Catholic, Protestant mainline, and Eastern Orthodox authors.

If you'd like to join the Brazos Book Club and receive our books upon publication at book club prices, please sign up online at **www.brazospress.com/brazosbookclub**.

To sign up for our monthly email newsletter, Border Crossings, visit **www.brazospress.com**. This email newsletter provides information on upcoming and recently released books, conferences we are attending, and more.

BrazosPress
The Tradition Alive